"Kelli Masters has an amazing story, and I'm so glad you all get to read about her commitment to her players and love for God. I promise this book will encourage you."

JASON ROMANO, host of *Sports Spectrum* and author of *The Uniform of Leadership*

"Kelli's story of sacrifice, humble beginnings, and laser focus is a true inspiration! In a culture where everyone is looking for a quick fix, *High Impact Life* reminds us how good old-fashioned hard work and determination pay off. Kelli's passion is tangible. Her desire to shine a light on the God-given talent in each of us will undoubtedly motivate readers to reflect on their own journeys. This book will challenge you to create a purpose driven game plan for success . . . and a much more fulfilling life."

ASHLEY BRATCHER, award winning actress, producer, and star of the box office hit *Unplanned*.

"Kelli Masters is one of top sports agents in the world, and I've been blessed to work with her and her athletes for over a decade. In this book, she shares her wisdom, insight, passion, and lessons on how to live a life worth telling a story about and ultimately create a High-IMPACT life. She's a true pioneer, and this book will motivate and inspire you to live your deepest purpose and best life. It's a MUST-read!"

TODD DURKIN, MA, CSCS; founder of Fitness Quest 10; author of *The IMPACT! Body Plan* and *Get Your Mind Right*; Lead Training Advisor & Ambassador of Under Armour

"*High-Impact Life* reads like an encouraging manual written by an old friend. Kelli effortlessly weaves the story of her life and faith, all while teaching you in the process. I have learned so much from her ground-breaking career that I can apply in my own life."

RACHEL JOY BARIBEAU, founder of #ImChangingtheNarrative and former national sportscaster

"Kelli Masters is a trailblazer whose life story is one of defying the odds, of success, and of having an indelible impact on everyone she meets. *High Impact Life* is an authentic behind-the-scenes playbook that will take you on an invigorating, faith-filled journey of stepping out in faith and stepping into your divine destiny. This book will help you elevate your thinking and inspire you to make the most out of every opportunity."

SCOTT WILLIAMS, CEO of Nxt Level Solutions, author, International Success Coach

HIGH-IMPACT LIFE

▲ ▲ ▲

KELLI MASTERS

HIGH-

A SPORTS AGENT'S SECRETS TO FINDING &

IMPACT

FULFILLING A PURPOSE YOU CAN'T LOSE

LIFE

TYNDALE
MOMENTUM®

The Tyndale nonfiction imprint

Visit Tyndale online at tyndale.com.

Visit Tyndale Momentum online at tyndalemomentum.com.

TYNDALE, Tyndale's quill logo, *Tyndale Momentum*, and the Tyndale Momentum logo are registered trademarks of Tyndale House Ministries. Tyndale Momentum is the nonfiction imprint of Tyndale House Publishers, Carol Stream, Illinois.

High-Impact Life: A Sports Agent's Secrets to Finding and Fulfilling a Purpose You Can't Lose

Copyright © 2021 by Kelli Masters. All rights reserved.

Cover photograph of stadium copyright © David Madison/Getty Images. All rights reserved.

Cover photograph of powder explosion copyright © Henrik Sorensen/Getty Images. All rights reserved.

Author photograph provided by author; used with permission.

Designed by Dean H. Renninger

Published in association with the literary agency of Legacy, LLC, 510 N. Orlando Avenue, Suite #313–348, Winter Park, FL 32789.

Unless otherwise indicated, all Scripture quotations are taken from the *Holy Bible*, New Living Translation, copyright © 1996, 2004, 2015 by Tyndale House Foundation. Used by permission of Tyndale House Publishers, Carol Stream, Illinois 60188. All rights reserved.

Scripture quotations marked NIV are taken from the Holy Bible, *New International Version*,® *NIV*.® Copyright © 1973, 1978, 1984, 2011 by Biblica, Inc.® Used by permission. All rights reserved worldwide.

Scripture quotations marked NKJV are taken from the New King James Version,® copyright © 1982 by Thomas Nelson. Used by permission. All rights reserved.

Scripture quotations marked KJV are taken from the *Holy Bible*, King James Version.

Some of the names and identifying details of individuals whose stories appear in this book have been changed to protect their privacy.

For information about special discounts for bulk purchases, please contact Tyndale House Publishers at csresponse@tyndale.com, or call 1-800-323-9400.

Library of Congress Cataloging-in-Publication Data

A catalog record for this book is available from the Library of Congress.

ISBN 978-1-4964-4453-0

Printed in the United States of America

27 26 25 24 23 22 21
7   6   5   4   3   2   1

CONTENTS

FOREWORD

Have you ever seen the first official photograph taken of
Margaret Thatcher and members of her Cabinet? At the
moment the image was taken, Thatcher had just been sworn
in as Prime Minister—the first woman to lead the govern-
ment of England in the more than one thousand years of its
history.

A casual glance at that captured moment reveals the
Prime Minister seated in the center surrounded by twenty-
four men, none of whom appear happy about the situation.
Only a few of the men are attempting a smile and one—
the third from Thatcher's right in the first row—is actually
scowling with his arms crossed.

Considering the monumental success Margaret Thatcher
achieved for Great Britain and the free world, the photograph
prompts me to laugh almost every time I see it. That image,
frozen in time, also reminds me of my friend Kelli Masters.

Considering the monumental success Kelli has achieved
for her clients and their families, plus her positive impact

on the NFL, Major League Baseball, the US Olympic Committee, and little girls everywhere . . . I can only wish there had been a snapshot taken that day in Washington, DC, when she took the exam for her sports agent license with three hundred men.

Better yet, I'd love to own a photograph of the moment six months later when Kelli walked into her first agent seminar at the NFL Combine. There, she was one of the only women among nine hundred men!

I first met Kelli a bit before she began the career transformation described in this book. Looking back now, knowing the pathway upon which she was about to embark, I can say with certainty that she was prepared—and not just intellectually. Kelli was ready in every way because she had so obviously worked on herself.

She had already completed a "life" transformation. By using every spare moment to read a wide variety of great books and by carefully seeking out wise mentors from whom she could learn, Kelli molded herself into the kind of person who succeeds in whatever he or she chooses to do.

As people read her "insider's account" of breaking into a tough but fascinating industry, I know they will enjoy the details of Kelli's story. It is my hope, however, that readers will also endeavor to mine these pages for the wisdom they contain and to understand what Kelli understands: She did not succeed because of who she was; she continues to succeed because of who she has become. And Kelli will be the first to tell you that she is still in the process of becoming!

I have worked with many different kinds of people during the course of my career. Those like Kelli, who work to intentionally develop a high emotional IQ, consistently fare better in whatever career path they choose. Kelli has a fun, resourceful, and persistent leadership style that's both clear and effective. In fact, she has now become the greatest kind of leader—a person whom others naturally want to follow. In an industry where suspicion seems the norm, where people are never surprised by a dirty trick, Kelli has become loved and respected. What does that tell you?

So now . . . read the book. You'll soon see why those of us who have watched Kelli through the years are proud of her. No one will ever give you more cause for great hope than this fine woman.

I consider it a privilege to know Kelli Masters and call her my friend.

Andy Andrews
New York Times bestselling author
of *The Traveler's Gift* and *The Noticer*

INTRODUCTION

SO . . . WHAT DO *YOU* DO?

It's mid-August and my flight to Seattle is completely full. In less than twenty-four hours, the preseason will kick off, and one of my clients will play in his very first NFL game.

Recruiting him has been an exhausting exercise—the research, the road trips, the meetings, the joy-filled days of extreme confidence, and the agonizing nights of self-doubt—but it's been so worth the effort in the end. We're about to experience the moment we've talked about since day one. My client is finally going to fulfill his lifelong dream—and, for the first time in what feels like months, I can finally relax.

As the plane settles in at cruising altitude, I reach over and pull down the window shade, hoping to take advantage of the long flight to catch a little much-needed sleep. But before I can close my eyes, the gentleman sitting next to me glances my way, smiles politely, and asks, "Are you going to Seattle for business or pleasure?"

I smile back. "Business."

He nods as he eyes my black ball cap, emblazoned with the "KMM Sports" logo. I know where this is going.

"So . . . ," he continues, "what do you do?"

I pause for a second as the familiar debate ensues in my head: *Should I just tell him I'm a lawyer, or should I tell him the whole truth?* I decide to come clean.

"I'm a sports agent."

His eyebrows shoot up. "Seriously? Like Jerry Maguire?"

"Yep."

"Wow. What sport?"

"Football, mostly," I respond.

He shakes his head. "Man, talk about a dream job!"

If you only knew, I think.

Actually, the *Jerry Maguire* comparison isn't that far off. In the movie, Jerry is an idealistic sports agent who ends up being fired from his large agency when he questions the dishonest way they do business. Down to two clients—one of whom coins the movie's most famous phrase, "Show me the money!"—Jerry is devastated when an unscrupulous agent, Bob Sugar, swoops in and signs one of them the night before the NFL draft.[1] While the movie has a happy ending, I still have a hard time watching it because it hits so close to home. I guess I've been "Bob Sugared" one too many times.

In real life, there's a lot more to my job than simply showing people the money, but like most people, my seatmate is more interested in the Hollywood angle: *What players do I represent? How many games do I get to go to every season? Do I stand on the sidelines, or do I get to sit in the owner's box? Do*

I get free Super Bowl tickets? Have I ever met Peyton Manning or Tom Brady?

Honestly, none of his questions bother me. A lot of people make assumptions about my job based on what they see on television shows and in the movies. In their minds, it's all champagne, limousines, and private jets. But the reality looks a little different (think fast food, hotel shuttles, and sleeping in airport terminals). And contrary to popular belief, I don't only go to football games and negotiate contracts. Though I can and have gone toe-to-toe with some of the best negotiators in the business, that's *not* why I became a sports agent. It was never just about getting the most money for my clients. My role extends far beyond that.

Truth be told, it's the part of the job nobody ever asks about that gives me the most joy. What I am most passionate about is helping my clients discover their God-given potential and putting them on the path to becoming everything He made them to be—not just in football but in life.

Most of my clients are only twenty-one or twenty-two years old when we meet for the first time, and up until that point, their entire lives have revolved around football. I want them to understand that they are more than that—that their value as human beings is *not* defined by what they do on the field.

From the very beginning of our relationship, we discuss the big picture. Who do they want to become? What kind of impact do they want to make—at work, in their community, and in the world at large? What legacy do they want to leave?

We talk about all of the opportunities that lie ahead of them, both during their football careers and afterward. I help them identify potential pitfalls and learn from mistakes others have made over the years. Together, we pray for wisdom, and we map out a plan that will allow them to pursue greatness in every area of their lives.

Maybe some of you grew up knowing exactly what you wanted to be, and that's what you became. If that's the case, that's amazing. But for most of us, the trajectory looks a bit different. Perhaps you had ideas about what you wanted to accomplish, but due to life circumstances, you ended up settling on a job or career track because it pays the bills. Maybe you felt pressured to carry on a family business that isn't exactly in your sweet spot. Maybe you took a job you didn't really want, never intending to stay long, but then you got comfortable. Now, years later, you're still there, feeling stuck. Or maybe you have specific passions or skills, but you have no idea how to channel them into a fulfilling career, ministry, or volunteer opportunity.

> *Your calling has nothing to do with being as good as or better than anyone else. It is about finding and fulfilling the purpose you were meant to serve.*

Regardless of where you are right now, please know this: You *do* have a calling, and that cannot be taken away from you, regardless of your circumstances, past mistakes, or what anybody else may say or think. Your calling has nothing to do with being as good as or better than anyone else. It is about finding and fulfilling the purpose you were meant to serve.

You are the first, last, and only you that has ever existed, and God gave you special gifts and talents for a reason. But *you* have to decide to walk out your divine calling and live out the mission you were born to fulfill. No one else on the planet can do what you were meant to do. It is up to you to take the necessary steps to become the very best version of yourself.

It is not going to be easy. In fact, when God calls you to do something, it may be harder than anything you would ever choose to do on your own. The only way you'll be able to accomplish it is with His help. But in the end, following God's call for your life is the only thing that lasts and the only thing that matters.

My goal is to do for you what I do with each of my athletes: to help you see who you truly are; to help you better understand the longings in your heart to accomplish more; to show you how to live a life that makes an impact; and to help you find fulfillment and purpose in your everyday life, starting right where you are.

So often we make inaccurate assumptions about ourselves. We beat ourselves up with negative self-talk. We compare ourselves to others and lose perspective. Sometimes we even lose hope. It's time to let go of all the things that keep us stuck in an unfulfilling place—fear, pride, confusion, weariness, and complacency. (Trust me, I've been there.)

You are fearfully and wonderfully made with unique gifts

that, when deployed with passion and consistency, will allow you to flourish in ways you've never imagined possible. It is time to discover your true calling and fully become the person you were created to be. It is time for you to live a high-impact life.

Kelli Masters

Chapter 1

THREE HUNDRED MEN AND ME

FINDING YOUR CALLING

"Excuse me, where is the ballroom?"

The young bellhop glanced up at me and smiled. "Just down those stairs, ma'am."

"Thank you!"

This was my first-ever stay at a five-star hotel (and, come to think of it, my *only*-ever stay at a five-star hotel), and my surroundings were both awe-inspiring and intimidating. I was at the Ritz-Carlton Hotel in Washington, DC, where approximately three hundred would-be agents would soon be put through a fast-paced review followed by a three-hour examination. I had studied and prepared for this moment for months. Well, I had prepared for the *test*. Nothing could have fully prepared me for the actual moment.

The stares.

The glares.

The whispers. "What is *she* doing here?"

A quick glance around the room confirmed I was the *only* woman taking the exam. Frankly, at that moment, I felt like the only woman for miles.

Most of the men looked to be around my age or younger, though there were a few "seasoned" individuals scattered throughout the room. I had purposely dressed professionally and conservatively because the last thing I wanted to do was draw attention to myself. But until that moment, the reality of the situation had escaped me. As a woman, I was alone in this quest. I was drawing unwanted attention to myself just by walking into the room.

As the stares and the whispers continued, I fought the urge to duck into the ladies' room and never come out. Instead, I scanned the rows of long tables and chairs filling the cavernous ballroom. Finding an open spot midway toward the back, I quickly made my way there and slid quietly into my seat.

Even though I felt anxious and alone, I certainly wasn't the only one feeling the heat. The pressure was on for all of us. We had already survived a months-long vetting process to get here. Once our applications had been approved by the NFL Players Association (NFLPA), we had each been sent a large stack of documents to study and an invitation to the "New Agent Seminar" (a misnomer since most applicants who attend the seminar *fail* the certification exam and don't actually become agents). We were about to complete the seminar, which was really just a review of the materials they had sent to us, and soon it would be time for the exam, a three-hour, multiple-choice test over every conceivable issue we would face as agents for NFL players—everything from the rules of free agency to what to do when a player gets injured or fails a drug test. The agent exam is given just once a year, and applicants have only two chances to pass before they are forced to wait another five years to reapply. So to say the mood in the room was tense is definitely an understatement.

Just as the NFLPA's director of salary cap and agent administration stepped to the platform to give a final overview of the collective bargaining agreement (the labor agreement between the NFL and the Players Association), a handsome young man with blondish hair rushed into the room carrying a large briefcase. He was dressed in a sharp gray suit and looked as if he had just escaped from some fancy Washington, DC, law firm. As he took the seat right in front of me, he glanced back, and I realized that I knew him. He had been a law school classmate of mine at the University of Oklahoma (OU). We had lost touch after graduation, when he left to take a job with the Department of Justice.

"Hey!" he said, smiling widely. "What are you doing here?"

"Oh, sports law is going to be a new practice area for me," I explained. "I didn't know *you* were going to be here!"

He went on to tell me how his brother, while in California

pursuing an acting career, had become friends with a number of high-profile college football players. That gave my former classmate the idea to branch out into agenting.

"We already have some clients lined up for when I pass this test," he admitted.

I smiled, but inside I shuddered. Suddenly it dawned on me that I had no future clients in the pipeline, no connections, and no idea how to even go about *making* connections. My confidence began to plummet.

"By the way," he asked casually, "did you study at all for this test? I haven't really had time."

"A little," I said, nodding. Actually, for the past several months, I'd done nothing *but* study for this exam. I'd pored over everything from split contracts and salary cap allocations to restricted free agency and everything else an agent needed to know in this industry. In order to become an NFL agent, candidates must have earned either a law degree or another graduate degree, and my Juris Doctorate and several years of experience practicing law had certainly helped me grasp the materials.

I'd felt prepared, but now fear and doubt started to creep in. *Even if I do pass this test, then what? Who are my future clients? How will I find them? How will I know what to do between finding those future clients and negotiating their contracts? And what happens after that?* Anxiety and a sense of personal inadequacy overwhelmed me. I closed my eyes and fell back in my chair.

How did I even get here?

THE MAKING OF AN AGENT

As a little girl, my earliest memories always involved football. In my home state of Oklahoma, football is king. Oklahomans plan their schedules and important life events according to the University of Oklahoma (OU) football season. For example, it is *not* okay to get married on the second weekend in October. That is OU/Texas weekend. Everybody knows it, and no one will come to your wedding. End of story.

As I grew up, my Friday nights revolved around high school games. In fact, if I close my eyes, I can still feel the crisp autumn air and hear the high school band and cheerleaders filling the night with cheers and chants. Saturdays were spent watching either OU or Oklahoma State play on television or listening to the game on the radio. On Sundays, my father's entire family would gather for a delicious potluck lunch at my grandparents' house. After lunch, we would watch either the Dallas Cowboys or Pittsburgh Steelers game on TV while my dad and his brothers napped on couches and recliners around the house and the cousins played football in the front yard.

On special Saturday mornings, we would go to Morgan's Bakery for doughnuts and watch our hometown parades with the high school marching band, majorettes, floats, and fire trucks. But on *really* special Saturdays, we would drive to the OU campus in Norman, Oklahoma, dressed head to toe in crimson and cream to watch the Oklahoma Sooners play in person.

After parking behind a stranger's house on Lindsey Street—usually right on their lawn, alongside other Sooner fans willing to pay an unreasonable amount of cash for a spot in a makeshift parking lot—we would fast-walk toward the towering football stadium. The sound of the drumline warming up on the lawn outside the stadium still rings in my head, and the smell of hot dogs grilling in the tailgate area beside the Duck Pond is burned into my memory.

To me, football game day was magical. The fans cheering, the band playing "Boomer Sooner" (OU's fight song) over and over and over, and the team rushing onto the field before the game followed by the famous Sooner Schooner— a covered wagon pulled by two ponies that serves as OU's official mascot. The pageantry of it all made my heart leap with joy.

My dad, who had played quarterback in high school and had been a play-by-play radio announcer since college, was exceedingly patient with my incessant questions. He sat my twin sister and me down at age five and gave us our first "chalk talk," explaining how the Xs and Os represented players and their movements on the field. From then on, I was hooked. I didn't want to be only an observer in the stands. I wanted to be out there on the field, involved in the action. I knew as a girl I couldn't actually play football, but still, the longing was there. I wanted to be part of the game, somehow, someway.

▲ ▲ ▲

After I finished my bachelor's degree in journalism at OU, I decided to follow in my father's footsteps and go to law school. I absolutely fell in love with it. Understanding the judicial system at a deeper level made me realize the power we have as Americans to fight for what is right and make a real difference in others' lives. Don't get me wrong, law school was incredibly difficult, and every single day was a battle. Many, many days I was ready to quit, but my deep passion for seeking justice saw me through.

After I graduated from law school, I became an associate at one of the largest and most prestigious firms in Oklahoma. My primary focus was on civil litigation, tackling complex disputes such as shareholder derivative suits and bad faith insurance claims. My life was dedicated to my craft, and my number one goal became making partner in my law firm. But while I knew I was good at my job, the subject matter of my cases—insurance, bank law, and business disputes—did not ignite passion within me. Instead, my fulfillment came from another area: nonprofit organization law.

While my litigation practice paid the bills, it was the work I did for charities, ministries, and other service-oriented organizations that filled my soul. Clients would come to me with a vision for making a difference in the world—feeding the hungry, fighting injustice, providing opportunities to those who had lost hope—and it was my responsibility to help make their vision a reality. They knew what they wanted to accomplish in the world; I knew how to prepare and file organizing documents, applications, policies, and bylaws to allow them to do it the right way. It was an honor to help others pursue their missions to impact lives around the globe, and my reputation as a skilled attorney who could help non-profits grew. Still, I felt as if everything I was doing was leading to something else . . . something even bigger.

In 2004, that "something" started to become clear when I connected with Josh Heupel. Josh was the quarterback who brought the OU football program back to prominence by winning the national championship in 2000. After a short stint in the NFL, Josh wanted to use his notoriety and influence to leave a legacy by helping needy families across Oklahoma and by setting up athletic camps for kids. He decided to do so through his own nonprofit organization, and thus "The #14 Foundation" was born. But issues arose that Josh and his family weren't quite sure how to handle, so they reached out to me for help.

So much of my career to that point had been consumed with trial law—civil lawsuits, fraud and defamation cases, contract disputes—in other words, people fighting with one another and relationships falling apart. Frankly, it was like a breath of fresh air to help someone whose dreams had come true with a foundation whose sole focus was helping others and building people up.

I met with Josh and his parents to discuss his goals for the foundation and get a clearer picture of the issues they were facing. From there, I helped them navigate all the necessary paperwork and legal red tape to ensure that both Josh and his foundation would be successful over the long haul.

In this role, I began to ask questions about other business and legal matters a professional athlete must handle—things like: "Who helps you set up your speaking engagements? Do you use a contract template? Who's in charge of negotiating your fees and making sure you get paid? Do you have an accountant? Have you set up an LLC yet?" The more questions I asked, the more I realized that many professional athletes are in way over their heads, *even if they've hired agents.* While players may have supportive families, they need the right advisers to guide them with wisdom and expertise on a multitude of legal and financial issues.

I spent the next several weeks walking the family through the process of revising policies and procedures for Josh's foundation, making sure that everything we did was in accordance not only with NCAA rules and regulations but with the state and the IRS as well.

At one point, Josh's mother looked at me, glassy-eyed, and said, "Where were *you* in the beginning? If you'd been an agent, we would have signed with you in a heartbeat."

I felt for her. Josh was still in his early twenties. He'd essentially gone from college student to CEO of his own company overnight. Sure, he had his parents to help guide him, but what he really needed was an attorney, an accountant, a financial adviser, and a business manager. A good agent would be able to fulfill those roles and help build a team of professionals around him. His situation made me think of all the other players and families out there who needed this help and also wanted to work with people they could trust . . . people who genuinely cared.

I'd never really thought about it before, but I realized that as soon as these young athletes get drafted or sign with a team, most of them suddenly find themselves with more money, choices, and influence than they've ever had in their lives. *Who helps them manage all of that?* I wondered. *Who helps them plan for the future? Protects them? Advocates for them? Makes sure they aren't taken advantage of? And what if they get injured? Who's helping them prepare for life after the NFL, helping them see how they can use their influence and platform to help others?*

That's when everything clicked. I could pool all the skills, knowledge, and experience I had acquired as an attorney with my passions for football and for serving others. If I became an agent, all of those things would combine to help me provide guidance and protection to young athletes like Josh.

By following my passions, I had found my calling.

Granted, not everyone was as excited about it as I was. When I shared my new career choice with my friends and colleagues, they gave me some . . . well . . . feedback.

"Why would you walk away from a great law practice?"

"Why would you start a sports agency in Oklahoma City? Don't you need to live in New York or LA to be a successful agent?"

"You should talk to other lawyers who have tried doing that. It's *impossible* to be successful in that business."

"You're going to lose more money than you make."

"What makes you think you could be a football agent? You've never played football."

And, of course, my favorite: "What do you know about football? You're a girl!"

In spite of their "support," I dug in and started doing extensive research, cold-calling every coach and athlete I knew and grilling them about their experiences dealing with sports agents. Unfortunately, most of them felt as though the agents they dealt with were largely in it for the money, focusing on the big names and ignoring the rest. The phrase I heard over and over again was "overpromised and under-delivered." And I couldn't find one person who said that his agent offered him any advice or preparation for life *after* football.

I also called countless agencies. The larger agencies didn't even respond. Most of the mid-level groups said they would only be interested in talking with me about being a client services assistant, marketing rep, or some other supporting role, not a certified agent. I knew working in that capacity wouldn't allow me to do the work I was envisioning.

And of course, I reached out to as many agents as I could find. Only one took my call—Kristen Kuliga. Like me, Kristen had started out as a lawyer, handling athletic marketing, sponsorships, and licensing deals for Woolf Associates out of Boston. When the founder retired, Kristen took on some of his clients, and in 2001, she became the first female agent to negotiate a starting NFL quarterback's contract when she brokered a $33 million deal between Doug Flutie and the San Diego Chargers.

We didn't talk long, but Kristen was incredibly helpful and encouraging. Still, her message came through loud and clear: I was going to face an uphill battle, and being a woman in a predominantly male industry wasn't going to make things any easier. Even so, I couldn't shake that feeling I got when Josh's mom looked up at me, completely overwhelmed, and asked, "Where were *you* in the beginning?"

What if Josh were my *son? What if any of the athletes I've spoken to over the past several months were mine? I can't even get these big agencies to return a simple phone call. Who's going to pick up the phone when one of these kids gets hurt or gets cut from a team or just needs help?*

Over the next several weeks, I created a business plan for starting my own agency, plus a financial document projecting how much money I would need to get me through the application and certification process. Then I pulled everything I had out of savings; borrowed the difference from friends and family, vowing to pay them back as soon as I could; and filed my application to become a certified agent.

I can still remember the way my hand shook when I signed the application and how I felt on that long, lonely walk to the mailbox. My critics' voices were echoing in my head, but with each step, the voices faded further and further into the background. As the envelope left my fingertips and disappeared into the mailbox, seemingly in slow motion, my destiny was set. There was no turning back.

EYES WIDE OPEN

Back in the ballroom, the proctor began passing out the certification exam booklets. As he placed the packet facedown in front of me, I closed my eyes and took a deep breath. In my mind, an unexpected vision emerged.

I saw a group of little boys, maybe six or seven years old, playing football in their backyard. They were just kids from the neighborhood, wearing no pads and using a worn, slightly deflated, kid-sized football, each one pretending to be his favorite player and fighting for the ball. Most likely they'd never seen an NFL game in real life. But they were playing—and dreaming.

As I watched, I sensed that, someday, those little boys were going to need me to guide them through the process of leaving college and playing in the NFL. They would need to know what to expect and how to prepare each step of the way. I would need to be there for them through the highs and lows, the major and minor decisions, the challenges brought on by becoming a professional in every sense of the word, and the difficulties that might accompany one day leaving the game behind. Those little boys and their families needed me to pass this test so that I would be prepared to help them realize their dreams and become everything God intended them to be.

In that moment, a sense of total peace washed over me.

The proctor's voice broke in. "You have three hours."

As I glanced up at the clock on the wall and flipped open

my exam book, all of the negative voices in my head began to fade away. I was *exactly* where I was supposed to be, doing *exactly* what I was born to do. And no matter what anyone else said or thought, that was all I needed to know. I had followed my passions, and they had led me to my true calling.

And nothing—literally, nothing—was going to stop me from fulfilling it.

PASSION + PURPOSE = CALLING

Though it's often described to me as a "dream job," becoming a sports agent was not something I ever intended to pursue. Even when *Jerry Maguire* first came out, I never once thought, "Hey—now there's something I'd like to try!"

Yes, I love football. And yes, I love the law. Both are passions of mine. But that's not why I became an agent. I got into agenting because I wanted to help young athletes make the difficult transition from college to professional sports. I wanted to help them understand that they are more than what they do on the field, and I wanted to help them see how they could use their unique gifts and platforms to positively impact others. Those are the things I value. Those are the things I cling to when the going gets tough. Those are the things that make what I do not just a job but part of a larger calling.

So what exactly is a calling? Growing up in the Bible Belt, I always thought of a "calling" as a super spiritual moment when the booming voice of God suddenly shattered the silence to tell you that you had been chosen to be a full-time pastor or missionary. Obviously, I figured, this only happened to certain, very special people. However, as I got a little older and my faith deepened, I realized that every human being has a calling—something that we were put on this earth to accomplish.

God gives each of us special skills, talents, and passions. Our job is to find a way to use them—not just for our own enjoyment but to help serve others and, in doing so, serve God. That added sense of purpose—that sense that you are contributing to something bigger than yourself—is what defines a calling. Passions are for your benefit. A calling turns those passions outward to benefit others.

Granted, the path may not always be as straight as an arrow. Goodness knows, mine wasn't. But if you continue to press in and follow your passions, God will point you in the right direction and show you what He's calling you to do. You just have to trust Him.

When I think about the path that led me to my career as a sports agent, I think of Proverbs 3:5-6: "Trust in the LORD with all your heart, and lean not on your own understanding; in all your ways acknowledge Him, and He shall direct your paths" (NKJV).

So often, we do lean on our own understanding. We look at the reality of our circumstances, and we apply our own reasoning and logic to those circumstances. We fail to trust and acknowledge God in the midst of it all.

But the truth is God loves us more than we will ever comprehend, and He cares about every detail of our lives.

He made us who we are. All the passions you have, all the dreams that are rooted deep within your heart—they're from Him. If you trust Him, He will lead you step by step as you pursue those passions. And in doing so, you will discover your calling.

Let me stop here for a moment and explain something. As you can probably already tell, my faith is very important to me, and my desire to fulfill God's calling on my life is at the core of everything I do. As I share personal experiences and important lessons in this book, I can't be fully myself without being transparent about my faith. But it is not my practice to expect everyone to believe exactly the way I do. I want you to be able to glean wisdom from these pages, whether or not faith is a part of your life. Yes, I am a Christian—a flawed human being who discovered God's love, mercy, and grace and, therefore, believes. Yet I have close friends and clients who are not Christians, and a difference in faith has never caused issues in any of those relationships because we show love and respect for each other. We learn from each other and grow.

As you read these chapters, my hope is that you will understand where I am coming from. Regardless of your spiritual beliefs, I hope you will receive what I have to say in a way that enhances your life and inspires you.

▲　▲　▲

When I first started thinking about becoming an agent, I wasn't sure I had what it took to make it. But the more I talked to family and a few close friends, the more they started pointing out all the ways God had been preparing me for this career from the get-go. I had a journalism degree, a law degree, and a background in athletics. (I trained and competed internationally in baton twirling for more than fifteen years—motivated in large part by my desire to be a part of the OU football experience. As an OU feature twirler, I had a chance to perform on the football field before each game and at halftime.) Thanks to an internship with a local CBS affiliate in college, I had experience working with the media. And, of course, as an attorney, I had loads of experience negotiating contracts and mediating between opposing parties.

Even then, as a natural introvert, I questioned whether I had the right personality for this job. But once again, my friends and family were quick to point out that even though I tend to be quiet, when I latch on to something, I become a fierce advocate. "Besides," they said, "you should see how your eyes light up when you start talking about doing this."

Eventually, I realized they were right. God had given me the training, the skills, and most of all, the passion. Even those around me could see it. I felt a confidence that I knew came from something bigger than me, and it showed.

WHAT DRIVES YOU?

What is it that motivates you each and every day? Is it primarily your paycheck? If so, it's okay to admit it. But the mere fact that you've picked up this book tells me that money isn't your only motivator. I don't know where you're at right now professionally, financially, emotionally, or spiritually, but I can promise you this: If you do not have a strong sense of purpose guiding your decisions, odds are whatever work you do will leave you feeling empty and unsatisfied—no matter *what* your paycheck says.

One of the things I always ask my clients when we first sit down together is "Who do you want to become?" Of course, the obvious answer is "A professional football player." But the shelf life of a professional athlete, especially in a heavy contact sport like football, is fleeting. In fact, it's not at all uncommon for NFL players to retire by the time they're thirty. The truth is most of my clients will spend more of their lives as *former* football players than they will as active players. And just as I commit to doing everything in my power to help them make the most out of their time in the league, I also want to position them to be equally successful *after* their NFL careers are over. That's why it's important to get them thinking about the big picture early and often.

Right from the start, I ask them what kind of impact they want to make on others and what legacy they want to leave. And yes, these are big questions—especially for a twenty-two-year-old whose entire life up to this point has been laser-focused on football. And yet in many respects, it's not all that different from asking a forty-five-year-old facing a career change what he or she wants to accomplish. When so much of your life has been spent pursuing one career path, thinking about doing something else can feel overwhelming, no matter how old you are.

So with my clients, we start small. We talk about things like: What makes you jump out of bed in the morning, excited to start the day? What keeps you up late at night, working for hours and hours without even realizing you're doing it? When you take breaks or need to clear your head, what do you find yourself thinking about, reading about, or doing? Or my personal favorite: If money were not an issue, what would you like to do for the rest of your life? The answers to these questions help you identify your passions.

But remember, it's not just about identifying what you're passionate about; it's also about discovering what fuels that passion.

In the case of my clients, if all they're passionate about is *playing* football, what happens after their playing days are over? They might fall into the trap of thinking that their best days are behind them or that there's nothing more they can contribute. But if we can tap into what it is about the game that they truly love, suddenly a whole world of opportunities opens up to them. A player who has a passion for strategy or game planning might go on to become a coach. Someone who has a knack for seeing talent in others might one day serve as a scout, identifying potential recruits. Someone who loves the fitness component of the game might find a rewarding second career as a personal trainer or even go back to school to study sports medicine.

The point is God gives these young men the passion and the skills they need to play professional football, but often-times, the experience they have in the league will shine a light on what they really love. Your passions and skills can do the same work of revealing what drives you.

FOLLOW THE PATH

A few years back, I represented a young running back out of Nevada named Stefphon. He wasn't chosen in the NFL draft, but he got picked up by the Tennessee Titans as a free agent. Unfortunately, he only lasted one weekend in training camp before being cut from the team. When I called him to deliver the news that his short NFL career was likely over (and yes, in case you're wondering, that *is* part of my job), I expected him to be devastated. After all, he'd been working for this opportunity his entire life. But he wasn't. In fact, he sounded more excited than he had the day the Titans signed him.

Why? Earlier that summer, I had taken a group of my clients on a mission trip to Haiti. I realize that may sound odd, but many of these young men were transitioning out of college into the intimidating world of professional football. As they prepared to report for training camp with all the experienced veteran players, they stood on the cusp of seeing whether their dreams would come true . . . or not. Most of these guys head into that first season feeling like they have the weight of the world on their shoulders. They're dealing with sky-high expectations from coaches, family, and friends; media scrutiny; and financial obligations they've never had to deal with before. Taking them to a developing country like Haiti, Rwanda, or Uganda gives them some much-needed perspective and a reminder of how much they really have been blessed.

We spent a lot of time during that trip talking about personal goals, the impact these young men's football careers would have on their relationships, and how to stay grounded and focused amid all the pressures and temptations they would experience as a result of who they are and what they do. I even brought along Brad McCoy, former coach and the father of NFL quarterback Colt McCoy, to teach some professional development and life skills sessions and to help lead Bible studies in the mornings.

Well, one day toward the end of the trip, Stefphon rushed over to me with a gigantic smile on his face and said, "Mama Kells, if I wasn't playing football professionally, I would want to do this!"

"Do what?" I asked him.

"This!" he repeated. "What you're doing. Helping athletes prepare for life after football. As soon as my NFL career is over, I want to go back to school, get my graduate degree, and help mentor young athletes."

Needless to say, I was floored. It was the most affirming thing I'd ever heard. The last time I spoke with him, he was in the process of becoming an associate athletic director with an emphasis on player development.

God gave him the passion and the skills to get into the NFL—if only briefly—and in the process of following that passion, he discovered his true calling.

I had another client, Cody, who also played for the Titans and made it through the entire preseason before being cut. He went on to play football in Europe and then briefly in

Canada before finally ending up in the Arena league, an American indoor football league, where he suffered a serious concussion that put the rest of his professional career in question.

As it happens, Cody was a strong Christian, and I'd heard him share his faith with teammates and at other events. Whenever he started talking about God, his eyes would light up, and he would completely come alive. So one day, as it started to become clear that his football career was winding down, I asked him if he'd be willing to do a few speaking engagements with Fellowship of Christian Athletes. Not only did he jump at the chance; he was great at it! People loved hearing him talk about his time in professional football, and sharing the peaks and valleys of his career gave him a humility and depth that made his message even more powerful. Today, that young man has a thriving career in public speaking and has impacted hundreds of thousands of lives around the globe.

Like Stefphon, Cody had a God-given passion for football that put him on the path. He followed where it led, and God did the rest. And He can do the same for you, too!

ASK. SEEK. KNOCK.

Odds are, you already have an inkling of what your passions and talents are. Be mindful of them and see where they take you—bearing in mind that your calling doesn't necessarily have to be a full-time job. Just because you love to bake doesn't mean you have to become a professional pastry chef to be fulfilled or to give back to others. Teaching a class at a local library, community college, or senior or rec center can be a wonderfully rewarding way to use your talents to help or inspire others. Love animals but not sure you're up to veterinary school? Try volunteering at a local shelter, getting involved with a program that helps train service animals, or helping at your local wildlife refuge. Enjoy playing the piano or guitar? Volunteer to play at church or at a local retirement center, give lessons to others, or make your own personalized recordings to share with family and friends. Whatever your passion is (and it may very well be a hobby you have right now), be deliberate

Whatever your passion is . . . be deliberate about nurturing it and looking for ways to expand it to have an impact beyond just yourself.

about nurturing it and looking for ways to expand it to have an impact beyond just yourself. You may even discover another passion in the process!

If you're not yet sure what your God-given passions or skill sets are, ask those around you. Sometimes friends and family can point out giftings that you never noticed, like I did for my client with the talent for public speaking. Listen to them. And try to stay open, even if what they are suggesting doesn't make sense at first blush. Looking inward is important, but sometimes the view from the outside is even clearer. Just as my friends noticed how much I lit up when I talked about becoming an agent, it will quickly become obvious to those around you when you discover your passion and begin to pursue it. Do not ignore those observations.

Some of my clients have been so hyper-focused on football that they haven't even had an opportunity to explore other areas of interest. In these cases, I have a special advisory council comprised of people from a wide variety of professions—such as Brad McCoy—that I offer up as mentors. These are people my clients can talk with to find out more about a given career, see if it might be a fit, and if so, decide what the next steps might look like, either now or a few years from now. Granted, there isn't a lot of downtime for professional athletes, but many players do take college classes or online courses during the off-season—sometimes to work toward finishing their degree and sometimes to test the waters in another area they've always been interested in.

If you're on the fence about a particular career, you might consider auditing an online course or enrolling in a night class. Maybe you've always enjoyed tinkering with cars but lack the formal coursework required to become a licensed mechanic. Maybe you have a flair for interior decorating or gardening but don't know the terminology or latest trends. Whatever your area of interest, odds are there is an online course, workshop, or seminar available to help you take the next step. Community colleges are often filled with people looking to start a second career or pursue a calling that had to be put on hold for one reason or another, so you'll probably find a few kindred spirits in the mix.

Also, don't be afraid to reach out and talk to others in your field of interest. Many people are more than happy to tell you about what they do, how they got involved in it, what they love about it, and what they don't. Listen to what they have to say. They may sour you on the idea completely (not all careers are as exciting as they look), or they may light a fire inside of you to take the next step!

Above all, ask God for wisdom and direction. After all, He's the one who created you and knows you best. Matthew 7:7-8 assures us that He will hear and respond when we approach Him: "Keep on asking, and you will receive what you ask for. Keep on seeking, and you will find. Keep on knocking, and the door will be opened to you. For everyone who asks, receives. Everyone who seeks, finds. And to everyone who knocks, the door will be opened."

IT'S NEVER TOO LATE

The bottom line is I encourage my clients to start thinking about their lives after football—asking questions and exploring opportunities early and often—and I encourage you to do the same as you think about what's next for you. And just as it's never too early to start thinking about who you want to be and what you want to accomplish in life, please hear me say this: It is *never* too late!

As long as there's breath in your body, you have the capacity to make an impact on the world around you. How and where is up to you. But be ready—the answer may surprise you. If you had told me twenty years ago that today I would be running my own sports agency, I would have laughed out loud. And yet, here I am, exactly where God wanted me to be.

So who do you want to become? What kind of impact do you want to make on others? What is the legacy you want to leave?

Do some soul searching. Think about the things that bring you joy and the things you're good at. Ask others what qualities or skills they see in you. Explore other opportunities and areas of interest. Start small. Keep your eyes, ears, and heart open. And most important, surrender your plans to God. He made you who you are, He knows who you will become, and He has already put you on the path to getting there. Trust Him—even when the path goes someplace unexpected. Remember that God doesn't waste anything. Every experience, every encounter, every peak, and every valley is there for a reason.

> *He made you who you are, He knows who you will become, and He has already put you on the path to getting there.*

I realize that may be difficult for you to believe, especially if faith in God has never played a major role in your life. But I truly believe that He does have a plan for every single human being on this earth—including you!

Jeremiah 29:11 says, "'For I know the plans I have for you,' declares the LORD, 'plans to prosper you and not to harm you, plans to give you hope and a future'" (NIV). I hope you'll come to believe that. I do, and I can honestly say that it has made all the difference as I have sought and found my calling.

Now let's get started. Your future is waiting.

DEVELOPING YOUR GAME PLAN

1. How might you answer a few of the questions I pose to my clients: *What makes you jump out of bed in the morning? What keeps you up late at night?* Or *If money were not an issue, what would you like to do for the rest of your life?* What might the answers to these questions reveal about your passions?

2. Reread Jeremiah 29:11. Do you believe that God has a plan for your life? If so, how does that belief give you an increased sense of meaning or purpose?

3. What are some gifts, talents, or passions others have noticed in you? Ask a few trusted friends, family members, or coworkers what strengths they see in you and how they think you might be able to use them to serve others. If they had to guess at your calling, what would it be?

4. One key question for all of us is this: *Who do I want to become?* Take a few minutes to consider your answer, and jot down the words that come to mind. What's one step you could take today toward becoming the person you want to be?

Chapter 2
GO FOR BROKE

GET READY TO MAKE
SOME SACRIFICES

"Are you sure you know what you're doing?"

I glanced across the table at my friend, and even with the bright Texas sun shining in my eyes, I could read the concern on her face.

If I had a nickel for every time a well-meaning friend or colleague asked me that question, I thought, looking down at my plate, *I would probably be able to pay for this meal.*

I folded my napkin and shot her a confident smile. "Positive." *Think she bought that?*

She held my glance for a second, then smiled and reached for her purse. "Okay, then. How much do you need?" she asked, producing her checkbook.

"About $1,800," I said, cringing. I hated having to ask for money, especially from friends, but one of my clients was going to be playing in the Super Bowl in two weeks, and I *had* to be there.

It was 2016, and almost ten years into agenting, I was *still* struggling financially. I was still working full-time at the law practice (and I mean FULL-time—many long days, late nights, and no sleep), but with most of my salary being poured into Kelli Masters Management (KMM), the sports agency I had started on my own, I had become something of an expert on "stealing from Peter to pay Paul." Every day brought with it a "Sophie's Choice" of sorts: *Do I pay my electric bill or get this client the new cleats he needs? Should I treat myself to hot water next month or pay my client's physical trainer for another week? Cable sports package or new receiver's gloves?*

I'd known going into it that starting my own sports agency was going to be an uphill battle—and an expensive one at that—but I had expected to be seeing a positive return on my investment by now. If anything, most days I felt like I was sinking even deeper into the hole.

I had made partner at my law firm at the end of 2005, and while the financial benefits were good, the position required a huge time commitment. I had been able to keep up with the heavy workload while also building my agency, but by 2012 it was virtually impossible to do both and do them well. So I gave up my partnership, which meant selling my shares back to the firm and taking an "of counsel" role with slightly better hours and more flexibility. It was a difficult decision to make, but I was finally signing players who were starting to stick in the NFL. Traveling around to all their games and scouting new recruits was taking more and more of my time, so I had decided to step back a bit from the law practice. Most of my colleagues at the firm had seen it coming. And most of them thought I was crazy for giving up a perfectly stable, well-paying partnership and sinking all my money into a bunch of twenty-year-old kids who might never be able to pay me back.

"Seriously, Kelli," I heard time and time again. "You should just drop this thing already. You could be making six figures and having a much easier life."

And you know what? They were right. When I think about all the time, energy, and money I've invested over the years, it makes my head spin.

Every player I represent requires an investment. It starts with the recruiting process—countless hours researching players, developing relationships, preparing presentations and materials, creating individualized game plans, driving or flying around the country to attend meetings and games— and I don't get paid or reimbursed for any of it. The investment only pays off *if* the player actually signs with me *and* makes it into the NFL. Even then, I get paid a very small percentage of the contract as a commission, and it can take several years to break even on a player when all the related expenses are factored in.

Let me step back for a minute to outline the process for those of you who might be wondering how exactly this all works—how a college athlete becomes a professional football player, and what role an agent plays in the process. It starts out with research. Agents evaluate players throughout their college careers, watching games, looking at statistics, and consulting with scouts to try to figure out which players are especially strong. Eventually agents begin talking directly with players, competing with other agents to sign them after their final college football season is over. That's because as soon as the Bowl Games end and the national championship game is completed, everyone's focus turns to the draft.

The NFL draft is held in April, and most players dream of being selected in one of the seven rounds—the earlier the better, at least in terms of salary, signing bonus, and the possible guarantees. A player wants to be in the best physical shape of his life that spring so he can make a good impression on coaches and scouts who evaluate players at events such as all-star games and the NFL Combine. The draft process is intense and fiercely competitive. Of more than 3,000 players eligible for the draft each year, only about 250 will be drafted, with some additional players being picked up as free agents. What's more, many of those players will end up being cut at the end of the summer when teams are required to significantly reduce their rosters. Their short NFL careers will end before the regular season even begins.

The odds of any player making it in the NFL are slim. My job is to try to figure out which players might succeed, decide which of *those* might be a good fit for me, and then recruit them by working to show each one that I'm the right agent to guide him through the process, negotiate his contracts, and support him through the whole journey.

Recruiting is not only expensive; it is also physically and emotionally draining. There have been times when I've driven eight or more hours for a meeting with a recruit, only to be stood up. I've flown across the country to sit and wait for a call that never comes. I've given exhaustive presentations to players, only to be told—to my face—that they would rather work with a less-qualified male agent than with a woman. On many occasions, I have invested resources, energy, and emotion with an athlete and his family for months or even years only to hear, "Thanks, but we are going in a different direction." Sometimes the no comes in the form of a phone call. Sometimes in a text. Sometimes it comes with no communication at all . . . just silence.

Of course, when a player and his family do say yes, it is a hard-fought victory! Time to celebrate, right? Yes, of course, but the time and expenses only increase. Every player I sign goes straight into a training program to get ready for the draft. These training programs, which I design for each individual athlete, include: physical and mental conditioning and preparation, coaching specific to the position they play, rehab or physical therapy, nutritional support, and everything else the athletes need to perform at their best during the draft evaluation process. That includes travel to the training location (usually Texas, Florida, or California), housing, rental cars, meals, and a stipend for living expenses. Most agents put together some variation on this plan, and the cost for each player can be as much as fifty thousand to one hundred thousand dollars. And that does not include my own time and expenses as I travel back and forth to check in on and support each of my draft prospects. All of this before we even get to the draft. And even then, there's no guarantee they'll get picked up—or stick.

OPPORTUNITY COST

A few years before I had to ask my friend to loan me the money for a Super Bowl ticket, I had signed a young player out of Texas Christian University (TCU). He was an outstanding college player. I'd gotten mixed reviews on him from the scouts I worked with, but I had been wanting to establish a pipeline into TCU for a while, and I was hopeful this young man might help me get a foot in the door. Immediately after I signed him, we flew to Miami so he could start training for his Pro Day, when NFL scouts would watch him work out with other players from TCU.

I arranged for him to work out at one of the top training facilities in the country; paid for a conditioning coach, a nutritionist, a massage therapist, a personal physician, and a position coach; set him up in a condo; and got him a rental car. Since he was no longer covered by his parents' health insurance, I also took care of that, got him whatever training equipment he needed, and gave him a weekly stipend to cover his food, gas, and other expenses.

I stayed in Miami for the first week to get him settled and then headed back to Oklahoma. He was in Miami for ten weeks, and we spoke practically every day. I would ask him how his training was going, we put together a wish list of teams he wanted to sign with if he entered free agency, and we talked about what to expect heading into the draft.

For the most part, my recruit was great throughout the whole process. I did notice, however, that he seemed to be blowing through his weekly stipend very quickly. One restaurant, in particular, kept showing up in his receipts. I'd been there once myself (and only once), and I knew it wasn't cheap. I often take clients out for a nice meal, and I let them order whatever they want while I just have a simple salad to make sure I can cover the bill. But this guy was really pushing the envelope with nice meals all the time. In fact, a few weeks in, he started asking for more money.

"Miami is really expensive," he told me.

"I realize that," I said. "But I've been looking through your receipts and you're going through your meal money *really* quickly," I countered, hoping he'd take the hint.

"Yeah . . . but I just *love* this restaurant."

Guess not.

Because his Pro Day workouts were quickly approaching, I opted not to make a fuss, and I upped his weekly stipend through the remainder of his training. That April, he attended invitation-only workouts for both the Cowboys and the Texans, and we headed into the draft hopeful that one of the two would make him a late-round pick—or, at the very least, sign him as an undrafted free agent.

Then the draft came and went. Nothing. Nobody picked

him up as a free agent, either. I called every contact I had in the league, trying to find him a spot somewhere, but I couldn't get a single offer. Two teams agreed to bring him in on a tryout basis, but neither one signed him.

Frustrated and disappointed, he fired me the next month.

I assured him that I still believed in him and that I wasn't ready to give up. "Teams pick up undrafted players over the course of the off-season all the time," I assured him.

No dice. He still wanted to part ways. Later that week, I sent him a letter outlining what he owed me. Needless to say, he was not happy. He sent back a lengthy text, the gist of which was "I can't believe you're trying to get money out of me."

I reminded him about our contract—one I use with all my clients, with terms that are standard for most agents. We had agreed up front in writing that I would pay for his training, but if he terminated our contract *before* he signed with a team, he would have to pay me back.

I closed my response with "I still believe in you." And I did.

That was the last I heard from him.

All told, I had invested upwards of thirty thousand dollars in him. All of it was lost.

While agents who lose money this way can go through the process of filing a grievance with the NFLPA and appearing before an arbitrator, it is often not worth the time. Collecting from the player—especially one who doesn't make an NFL roster—is very difficult. And if an agent earns any commission from a player, arbitrators tend to see the agent's expenses as a "cost of doing business" and won't enforce the contract, even though it is a legally binding agreement.

I'd love to say this was the only time I invested tens of thousands of dollars in a client only to wind up in the red, but it's not. There have, unfortunately, been many times where I've fronted all the money for a client's training only to have him scooped up by another agent, leaving me high and dry.

And it's not just a question of money; it's also a question of time.

The fluid nature of the job means that I need to be willing to drop everything on a dime. If I go out to dinner with friends and get a call from a client, I have to take it. I haven't had a legitimate vacation since college, and I can't make any family commitments around holidays. In fact, since becoming an agent, I've missed practically every holiday family get-together. Most of my Thanksgivings are spent at a stadium somewhere, eating whatever the vendors are hawking that day or whatever I can dig up at the airport. Most Christmases are spent accompanying my clients to children's hospitals or other charity events, and most New Years are spent on the recruiting trail, traveling back and forth to Bowl games my potential recruits are playing in.

The point is following my calling as an agent has proven both costly and time-consuming. I have slept in my car and in baggage claims more times than I care to count. And I ate more boxed macaroni and cheese and Top Ramen as an adult with a law degree than I did as a college student. But to me, every sacrifice has been worth it. This is what God put me here to do, so whatever it takes to fulfill that calling, I am willing to do it.

Fortunately, my ramen noodle days are behind me. But when your road to success is difficult and demanding, you appreciate the wins far more. I know this: I truly treasure every happy moment. Sometimes it is standing on the sidelines during pre-game warm-ups and seeing one of my players run toward me to give me a big "Thank you for being here!" hug. Sometimes it is finalizing a life-changing contract for a player, one that he never dreamed he'd earn. Other times it's a simple call or a note from a parent, a coach, a fan, or a young aspiring agent, reminding me of the impact I've had on a life. The rewards that come from a willingness to make sacrifices are far more than financial.

YOU GET OUT WHAT YOU PUT IN

Pursuing your calling may require a great deal of personal sacrifice. Depending on what you feel called to do, you may have to quit your job, go back to school, relocate, rethink your financial portfolio, or give up precious time with family and friends. But here's the thing: If it's your calling—if it's who you are and what you were put on this earth to do—it won't *feel* like a sacrifice. It will feel like a privilege. That's how you know your calling is real.

When it's your calling, difficult decisions (like my forgoing hot water so a client I believe in can get the training he needs) are not *have* to's; they're *get* to's. You make these decisions not because it's what you *do* but because it's who you *are*. It's how God wired you.

> *When it's your calling, difficult decisions . . . are not have to's; they're get to's.*

Why do first responders rush into burning buildings when everyone else is running the other way? It's who they are. It's how they're wired. The sacrifices they're willing to make may not make sense to anyone else around them. Yet if you were to ask them, they'd likely tell you they can't imagine living any other way. I've been agenting for almost twenty years now, and well-meaning friends and colleagues *still* remind me repeatedly that I could make a lot more money practicing law. But what they don't understand is that I don't do what I do for the money. If that were the case, I would have packed it in years ago. I do it because I truly believe this is what God has called me to do.

You'll often find that committing to something bigger than yourself affects more than just you. Sometimes pursuing your calling can impact your family and friends as well. I have known countless coaches and players who have had to uproot their entire family multiple times as a result of trades or team personnel changes. Kids have had to change schools. Spouses have had to leave jobs, friends, and churches behind. It's not always easy. But then, nothing worthwhile ever is. As you make decisions and get buy-in from your family, the question you need to ask is "Are we willing to make those sacrifices?"

A few years ago, I represented a young man who was strong, fast, uniquely gifted, and drafted by the Detroit Lions.

I attended rookie orientation meetings with him. We found a great house for him to rent outside of Detroit but not too far from the Lions facility. He even bought a nice new Cadillac with part of his signing bonus. It seemed as if everything was falling into place for him. But once he got to training camp, everything started to fall apart.

One day he called me and said, "I can't do it anymore, Kelli. I just can't." When I pressed him for more information, he told me, "I hate getting up early in the morning and having to work all day. I'm tired of the pressure and never feeling like I'm good enough." Then he sighed, fell silent for a moment, and said, "It's just a lot of work."

"Listen," I said to him. "For the rest of your life, you're going to have to do a lot of work. Whether it's playing football or digging ditches, you're going to have to set an alarm clock, get up, and go to work—everybody does."

"Kelli," he said, "I just want out."

"Please listen to me," I urged. "You don't want to quit . . . not really. You're going through a tough time, but I promise if you just keep going, you're going to be fine. Think of how badly you wanted to be where you are now. Think of how hard you've worked. How much you've been through. Think of all the people out there who would give anything to be in your shoes right now.

"I promise you," I cautioned him, "your life is not going to get any easier if you quit."

I managed to convince him to stick it out a little while longer, hoping that once the football season started, his natural passion for playing would kick in and he'd be fine. It didn't happen. He started blowing off team meetings and showing up to practices late, and as a result, he wound up spending most of his game time on the sidelines as a healthy scratch, meaning he didn't even get to suit up for the game.

I traveled to Detroit regularly to be by his side. That Thanksgiving, instead of enjoying a lovely holiday dinner with friends and loved ones, I found myself choking down a hot dog at Ford Field, watching him stand on the sidelines during the Lions game. After the game, we went to Ruth's Chris Steak House for dinner (I paid, of course) and then to one of his favorite dive bars to play pool, where—not to brag—I beat him two games out of three.

We talked about the struggles he'd been having, and he complained about how hard it was to have to get up early every day and go into the facility not knowing if he was even going to get to play.

"You don't *have* to be there," I corrected him. "You *get* to be there." I reminded him how many college players dream of being part of an NFL team and don't make it, yet God had given *him* the skills required to turn that dream into a reality. "You've been given an amazing gift," I told him. "Please don't throw it away."

Unfortunately, as much as I wanted him to reach his goals

and realize his fullest potential, he just didn't want it for himself. Correction: He wanted it. He just wasn't willing to do what it took to achieve it.

Sadly, it came as no surprise when the Lions' personnel director called a few months later to let me know my client was being released from his contract and wouldn't be on the team next season. To this day, he is one of the strongest, most naturally gifted athletes I've ever represented. And to this day, it pains me to think about where he could have been compared to where he is now.

A lot of people dream of becoming professional athletes, musicians, or artists, but they simply don't have the natural talent to make it happen. That's why when we *are* given a great gift, it is almost a crime not to make the very most of it.

God gives us each special gifts and callings, tailor-made for us. He wants us to use and pursue them not just for our own benefit but also for the benefit of others. Will there be sacrifices involved? More than likely, yes. But remember, it's not just about you. You have the potential to impact countless others, some of whom you may never even meet. What a shame it would be to throw that opportunity away. Who knows what kind of impact this young man's career might have had on other young athletes, his family, or his community? That's why when God calls us to do something, I believe we have a responsibility to act.

UNIQUELY CHOSEN

Some of the greatest sources of inspiration in my life are stories of others who faced unthinkable difficulties yet rose to the challenge and succeeded. As it happens, many of the most profoundly impactful stories I have found are from the Bible. Scripture is full of accounts of ordinary human beings who, with God's help and through faith and perseverance, overcame extraordinary circumstances to fulfill their callings.

One such person is Esther, whose life is the subject of an entire book of the Bible. Interestingly, the book of Esther never mentions God by name. However, we can see Him working behind the scenes through a young woman who simply said yes to a greater purpose—even if it meant sacrificing her own life.

The Old Testament book of Esther takes place during a time when many of the Israelites had been exiled from their country and resettled in surrounding lands. Esther was an orphan, raised in Persia by a cousin who served in the king's court. When King Xerxes decided to select a new wife from the women of his empire, his servants gathered up all the beautiful young women in the region, including Esther. Each woman received twelve months of beauty treatments and "her choice of whatever clothing or jewelry" before being presented to the king (Esther 2:13). It was kind of like Miss America (or in this case, Miss Persia) meets *The Bachelor*, except in this case, the winner got to become the king's bride *and* be crowned queen.

When it came time for Esther to be presented, she so captivated the king that "he set the royal crown on her head and declared her queen" (2:17). But this was not your typical love story. In fact, Esther was not even allowed to approach her new husband unless he called for her. The penalty for doing so was death. But even in this situation, Esther had an important calling to fulfill. She had been placed by God into a position of great influence not for her own benefit but to help others—indeed, to save their lives.

You see, not long after she married the king, Esther was made aware of a plot to kill her people, the Jews. She knew that she had to speak to the king in order to save her people, but she also knew that if she went to him uninvited, she could be killed. Yet despite the risk to her own life, Esther chose to enter the king's inner court. She sent a message to her cousin Mordecai, declaring, "If I perish, I perish" (4:16, NIV).

Talk about bravery! She knew full well that approaching the king without permission could be a death sentence, but her belief in her calling was stronger. She could have closed her eyes to her people's suffering and stayed safe in the palace, yet she chose to risk it all, knowing she could be sacrificing her comfort, her status, and even her life. She realized that, as her cousin Mordecai prophetically stated, she had ascended to this position as queen "for such a time as this" (4:14, NIV).

God had put Esther exactly where he needed her. He had given her the beauty and the character to win the king's heart, the wisdom to discern the right thing to do, the courage to speak out, and the faith to believe that her obedience would be rewarded. And it was. The king listened to Esther, and the Jewish people were spared.

God willing, you and I will never have to face the kind of life-or-death decision Esther did. And yet sacrifice, even a less onerous one, is a key component to reaching any goal. Without pain, there is no growth. Without setbacks, there is no perseverance. Without delays, there is no patience. Every single imperfect, unpleasant, or seemingly unbearable moment in your life gives you an opportunity to either give up or grow. But you get to choose . . . always.

> *Every single imperfect, unpleasant, or seemingly unbearable moment in your life gives you an opportunity to either give up or grow.*

Every day of your life, the choice is yours: Will you embrace the demands, the discipline, and the sacrifices that will lead you to an impactful and ultimately fulfilling life? Or will you complain, grow bitter, give up, and feel sorry for yourself? I wish I could say I never complain, but I have my weak moments. We all do. The key is to refuse to let yourself stay there.

Whenever you find yourself slipping into a negative place because of the sacrifices you're facing, shift your focus to what makes you grateful (think of all the "*get* to's"). Meditate on the blessings in your life and the gifts you have been given, and visualize yourself moving *toward* your goals and dreams. And remember, as long as you are actively and obediently following God's calling for your life, you will always be on the right path. It may not always be the easiest path, but it will always be the right one.

DEVELOPING YOUR GAME PLAN

1. What sacrifices have you had to make for a job, a dream, or a relationship? Which of these were the hardest for you, and which were the easiest? How could thinking, *I get to do this* rather than *I have to do this* change the way you think about hard work and sacrifice?

2. Do you agree with the statement "Quitting won't make your life any easier"? What helps you persevere when you're tempted to quit? How can we gain perspective when we feel like quitting something that's important to us?

3. Esther knew that she had become queen not for her own personal benefit or comfort but to help her people. How did this knowledge enable her to act sacrificially? If we understand our own callings as opportunities for service, how might we be encouraged to give up some things for the greater purpose we were born to fulfill?

4. As you continue to consider what your calling might be, what are a few goals that could help you take another step toward that calling? Write these down, along with a list of reasons these goals are important to you, and reread them when you feel discouraged and wonder whether your effort is worth it.

Chapter 3
EVERYONE'S A CRITIC

SURROUND YOURSELF
WITH WISE COUNSEL

I arrived in Indianapolis for my first NFL Combine on a blustery Thursday afternoon in February of 2006. I had been a certified agent for just six months, and I only represented one client at the time: Cody Hodges, a young quarterback out of Texas Tech. Though he had a lot of natural talent, Cody had not received an invite to the Combine, so I was there alone to attend the agent seminar. Well, not completely alone. I was surrounded by agents, most of whom had been in the game a lot longer than I had. Some had client lists as long as your arm, and some were almost as well-known in NFL circles as the superstars they represented. And in what was becoming an all-too-familiar experience, there was not another woman in sight. Being a natural introvert, I had to force myself out of my hotel room and into the throng of testosterone that seemed to fill every hotel lobby, restaurant, and bar within a square mile. To say that it was intimidating would be a massive understatement.

The annual Combine is a huge deal for the more than three hundred college players who are invited. First they endure long hours of medical evaluations, formal interviews, and mental examinations. Then they demonstrate their speed, strength, skill, and athleticism by performing drills—which are broadcast live on national television—for NFL scouts and coaches. It all happens just two months before teams finalize their draft picks. But the Combine is also an important professional gathering for agents, who are there to attend training seminars, to network, and to advocate for their clients. It's an immensely competitive environment where everyone is concerned about who they've signed and what their prospects are for the draft.

As I made my way to the seminar, my confidence began to wane. *What am I doing here? What if everyone's right? What if trying to be an agent is a mistake?*

With each step I took, my heart pounded even harder in my chest. Picking up my badge from the welcome table and putting on my best game face, I strode into the ballroom and surveyed the layout. Approximately nine hundred chairs were set up at long conference tables, sprawling across the room in three sections. At the front, a stage was adorned with a giant NFLPA logo, a podium, and a table draped in black and topped with three microphones and a pitcher of water. I slid into a seat at the left end of the center section, near the back.

I closed my eyes and took a deep breath. *You're here. You belong here. You can do this.*

It was going to be a long day.

Throughout the course of the morning, speaker after speaker addressed the room about key NFL policies such as the salary cap, franchise tag numbers, player benefits, and agent discipline. It was information I knew well, thanks to my preparation for the agent exam. With only one client, though, still undrafted, I had yet to actually use any of it.

At one point during the seminar, I got up from my chair and exited the ballroom. I honestly just wanted to get away from that environment for a moment, so I headed straight for the ladies' room. *At least there won't be a line,* I laughed to myself.

On my way, I noticed a group of reporters gathered around a man who looked to be in his late forties and seemed to exude confidence and charisma. The reporters held tape recorders up to his face and were quizzing him about a player. Reporters are not allowed into the actual agent seminar, so they typically wait outside, hoping some of the agents will come out and either divulge whatever is being discussed or reveal some inside information about one of their clients. From the level of attention the reporters were giving this man, I assumed he was an agent who represented a high-profile draft prospect.

As I passed the group, I glanced over at him. As soon as we made eye contact, he pushed his way through the bevy of reporters and strode right over to me. He had what struck me as a rather cocky grin on his face.

"What are you doing here?" he asked accusingly. Then, before I could answer, he added, "How many clients do you have?"

His tone caught me completely off guard. I paused for a second and collected myself. Then, with all the bravado I could muster, I said, "I'm an agent—like you. And I have one player."

I sincerely hoped that sounded more impressive to him than it did to me, but the snide expression on his face assured me it didn't.

"Let me tell you why you don't belong here," he said. "Women will never make it in this industry." You could cut the condescension with a knife. As an added bonus, he said it just loud enough to draw his media throng nearer. I could have sworn I heard one of the reporters snicker.

Turning my attention back to him, I asked, "Can you please tell me your name?"

When he told me who he was, I realized I was being lectured by one of the most well-known agents in the industry. I didn't recognize his face, but his name had been on many of the player contracts I had studied. And now he was telling me why I never would be a success in this industry—in front of the media, no less.

"Players will never respect you. Coaches won't listen to you. General managers won't want to talk to you. It's just never going to happen."

Wow, I thought. *Did he prepare this speech ahead of time?*

"You should find something more appropriate to do with your life," he continued, "because mark my words, you will not be successful here."

I was surprised he didn't add "honey" or "sweetheart." I could feel the heat rising in my face and up the back of my neck, and for a minute I couldn't tell whether I was going to cry or start shouting at him. Then, out of nowhere, a peace came over me that I can only attribute to God.

"Are you finished?" I asked. He just stared at me incredulously.

"Good," I said before he could start in again. "Because let me tell you why you're wrong." I took a slight step forward, forcing him to step back. "You don't know me. You don't know why I'm here. You don't know what I'm capable of. And mark *my* words," I said, pointing at his chest for effect, "you are going to have to deal with me someday!"

And with that, I turned on my heel and was—I suspect—halfway to the ballroom before his jaw snapped back shut.

Though I had neither the evidence nor the experience to prove it, I just knew this man was wrong. I knew I was supposed to be there. And even if this guy disagreed, I knew I would be successful.

DON'T DO ANYTHING RASH

Sadly, the early days of my agenting career were jam-packed with doubters, critics, and naysayers. And the higher the stakes got, the louder those voices became. But I was fortunate that even with all the cynics whispering doom and gloom into my ear, I also had cheerleaders in my life reminding me of all the unique, God-given gifts and abilities I brought to the table.

One of those encouragers in my corner was a man named Terry Tippens, a senior partner at my law firm. Terry believed in me from day one. He is one of the most accomplished and respected trial lawyers ever in Oklahoma, a staunch advocate for his clients, a creative "think outside the box" litigator, and a genuinely likable guy. (He also raised cattle—a real-life Oklahoma cowman.) When I was fresh out of law school, Terry took me under his wing and gave me a rather daunting assignment, one meant for a much more experienced lawyer. He believed in me before I believed in myself as an attorney. And he continued to believe in me over the years, even when I launched my sports agent career against the odds. "If anybody is capable of succeeding in this business, it's you," he assured me. I've never forgotten his unwavering support. He was one of the few positive voices early on.

It seems to be one of the indisputable laws of human nature that as soon as you start talking about your calling with others, they will start sharing their opinions of it with you. And if you don't know how to handle that, it can be dangerous. Too much negativity and your confidence might start to waver. Too much blind support and you might rush headlong into a bad decision. Yet as tempting as it may be to tune out everyone else and just go with your gut, making critical life decisions in a vacuum can yield equally disastrous results.

I had one client, an offensive lineman out of Texas, who signed with the Patriots, got cut in training camp, was picked up by the Browns, and then got cut a few weeks later—only to have the Patriots express interest in him again.

When I called to tell him he had a flight back to Boston, he said, "I'm not going. I'm tired of getting my head beat in at practice every day for nothing. It's just not worth it."

"Well," I said calmly, "that's your decision. I'm not going to force you into anything, but please—sleep on it, pray about it, talk to your family. This is a big decision," I cautioned him. "If you tell the Patriots no and walk away, that's it. Nobody else is going to be willing to take a chance on you."

But he was adamant. He was tired, he was frustrated, and he wanted out. A year later, he called me in a panic.

"Kelli, I made a mistake. Can I get back in?"

"I'm afraid it's too late," I told him. "I'm sorry." And I was. Had this young man taken the time to pray about the decision or to consult with his family, he might still be playing in the NFL. But he let his emotions get the best of him, shut everyone else out, and, in the completely wrong frame of mind, made a decision that impacted the rest of his life.

Proverbs 15:22 says, "Plans go wrong for lack of advice; many advisers bring success." As both a Christian and an attorney, I believe that wholeheartedly. As difficult as it can sometimes be to discern good advice from bad advice, or to have someone else criticize your ideas and decisions, the truth is you will almost always regret any decision you make

You will almost always regret any decision you make in a vacuum.

in a vacuum. As we've already established, pursuing your life calling may require some hefty sacrifices, and the decisions you make can affect more than just you. That's why I always advise my clients to seek counsel before making any major decisions. Of course, who you choose to both talk *and* listen to can make all the difference.

I THINK YOU NEED TO SEE A COUNSELOR

At the beginning of their professional careers, most of my clients are so young and impressionable that it's hard for them to figure out who they can trust. They are, as a lawyer would say, "unsophisticated." (I really don't care for this term, by the way. My clients aren't cavemen. They just don't have any formal experience in business.) That doesn't mean they should live in a constant state of paranoia, but a healthy dose of skepticism *can* be a good thing—especially if it encourages them to hit the pause button, step back, and take the time to discern good advice from bad advice.

One of the things I love about being a lawyer is that we're often referred to as counselors (as in: one who provides legal counsel). When someone comes to us with a problem, we don't just toss out advice willy-nilly or offer our personal opinions. We carefully weigh all the available information; consider the situation, the risks, and the alternatives; and then provide a sound, well-reasoned course of action. Our conclusions may not always be what our clients want to hear, but they will always be in our clients' best interests.

Many young players and their families are easily bamboozled by agents because everything they're told during the recruiting process sounds so good: *I'll get you a huge contract. Stick with me, and you can write your own ticket.* Unfortunately, there is so much corruption and deceit in this business that unless a family really digs for information, they can easily be blindsided.

When my clients are seeking or receiving advice, I always counsel them to carefully consider the source. Ask yourself, *Can I genuinely trust this person? Do I know them well? Do they know me well? What is their agenda? What do they stand to gain—or lose—from "helping" me?*

Above all else, look for people who are willing to tell you the truth—not just what you want to hear. The best advisers are people who not only love you as you are but love you so much that they want to see you become the best you can be. More often than not, that means family, close friends, and, if you are a person of faith, God.

> *The best advisers are people who not only love you as you are but love you so much that they want to see you become the best you can be.*

When I am trying to make a decision with major consequences, I most often talk to my husband, Dale. We were friends long before we married, and I have always trusted his wise counsel and discernment. He helps me process all of the options and consider the obstacles I may face. I am incredibly thankful for his wise counsel, as well as the input of other trustworthy advisers. But I never make a major life decision without first spending time in prayer. After all, nobody knows what's best for me or has my best interests at heart more than the One who created me. I also spend time reading His Word, which I like to think of as an instruction manual for life, filled with divine wisdom and insights to provide guidance when I'm not sure what to do. Reading the Bible and spending time in prayer helps me drown out the competing thoughts and voices in my head and makes it easier for me to discern what the prophet Elijah referred to as "a still small voice" that I know is God guiding me (see 1 Kings 19:12, KJV).

When I talk to my clients about this part of the process, I sometimes refer to it as "centering" yourself. That means shutting out all outside distractions, quieting the voices in your head, and focusing on finding your center—that place where you feel completely at peace and can sense God's guidance as He shows you the path more clearly. It has been my experience that when you are truly at peace with a decision, more often than not, it's the right one.

WEIGHTY DECISIONS

As odd as it may sound, one question almost all of my players ask me as they head into the draft is "What should my weight be?" Because height and weight are so heavily evaluated in the NFL, when the Combine rolls around, every team puts their prospective players up on stage and weighs and measures them in front of everyone. While there's nothing you can do about your height, a lot of players will make a concerted effort to either gain or lose weight prior to the draft to improve their chances of getting picked.

The problem is, every year, every team will be looking for something different. A team looking to build a faster, more agile defensive line might want a leaner, more muscular lineman, while a team looking to create a wall might be looking for a stouter, more substantial lineman. The same can be said for virtually every position on the field. Some teams want strength and bulk; some want speed and agility; all want some combination of the two. At any given Combine, I could ask scouts from all thirty-two teams their opinions on a player's ideal weight and not find a consensus.

That said, I try to give my clients a range, based on where I think they have the best chance of being picked up, to use as a baseline. After that, I tell them it's up to them. They have to decide at which weight they feel the strongest and the fastest and at which weight they truly feel they are at their best—not because it's what the Jaguars want, what the Jets said, or what the Giants need, but because it's what makes the most sense for them.

When you're seeking counsel for your own big decisions, remember that you're not asking someone to make a decision for you. If that were the case, I would have walked away from agenting in the middle of that first seminar. You're merely collecting information from trusted advisers to help you discern what is best for you. The final decision is—and always will be—yours. Don't let anyone take it away from you.

SOMETIMES THINGS CAN GET A LITTLE HAIRY

You may have heard the name Samson before. He's that giant, muscular guy from the Bible who's often depicted pushing apart two crumbling pillars. He's also a perfect example of what can happen when we listen to the wrong people and stray from our God-given calling.

We meet Samson in the Old Testament book of Judges, which takes place in the years after the Israelites crossed over to the Promised Land. They were being oppressed by the Philistines, a neighboring people who fought against Israel for generations. Samson's mother, whose name we aren't given, had been unable to have children, but one day an angel appeared to her and told her she would give birth to a son. Not only that, he told her that her son would be "set apart" to deliver God's people from their enemies, the Philistines. He also instructed her never to cut the boy's hair.

As foretold, the woman gave birth to a son, whom she named Samson. Samson quickly grew big and strong and rose to a position of leadership among the Israelites, his long, uncut locks a tangible symbol of his obedience to God.

Samson's supernatural feats of strength are well-documented—he destroyed Philistine crops; killed one thousand Philistines with the jawbone of a donkey; and carried away the gates of Gaza when his enemies tried to trap him inside the city. But, like most people, he also had weaknesses—in particular, beautiful women.

Enter Delilah.

Delilah was a Philistine woman who captured Samson's heart so instantly that we can only imagine she was stunningly beautiful. Unfortunately, Delilah was also greedy and conniving. When the Philistine rulers offered her 1,100 pieces of silver each if she could get Samson to divulge the source of his superhuman strength and how it could be overcome, she used all of her feminine charms to entice him into telling her.

The first few times Delilah asked him what made him so strong, and what it would take to keep him securely bound, Samson lied. So when the Philistines tried to capture Samson using the techniques Delilah gave them—first tying him up with new bowstrings, then new ropes, then weaving his long braids into a loom—they failed.

Still, Delilah continued to press him. And even though Samson had to have known by now that Delilah was not to be trusted, he finally succumbed and told her the truth: "My hair has never been cut, . . . for I was dedicated to God as a Nazirite from birth. If my head were shaved, my strength would leave me, and I would become as weak as anyone else" (Judges 16:17). That night, "Delilah lulled Samson to sleep" and then brought someone in to shave his head (16:19). The next morning, when the Philistines attacked, Samson was unable to fight back. Because of his disobedience, "the LORD had left him," and the Philistines "gouged out his eyes" and took him captive (16:20-21).

But the story doesn't end there. At a religious festival for their god, Dagon, the Philistines decided to bring Samson to their temple so they could gloat over their victory and proclaim the superiority of their god. In Samson's final moments, as he was standing between the pillars of the Philistine temple, he called out to God, "O God, please strengthen me just one more time" (Judges 16:28). God answered his prayer, filling him with such strength that Samson was able to bring down the temple in one final act of bravery. He lost his life, but so did the thousands of Philistines gathered in the temple. That moment led to God's people being delivered from their enemies, just as the angel had foretold.

Even though Samson listened to and trusted the wrong people, bringing about his own suffering as a result, God remained faithful, and even in his death, Samson fulfilled his calling.

KEEP THE FAITH

God will always remain faithful—even when we aren't. If He has called you to do something and has given you the giftings, skills, and passion with which to do it, He will guide you along the way. He will be there for you, even when things don't go as planned. So keep the faith. Even when I find myself eating cheese and crackers for dinner in an airport terminal on New Year's Eve on my way to meet with a prospective client who may or may not decide to sign with

KMM, I can rest confidently in the knowledge that I am exactly where I am supposed to be, doing exactly what God has called me to do. It's not about our glory; it's about His. Our job is simply to trust in God and follow wherever He leads us.

No matter what question or challenge you're facing—*Should I bulk up or slim down? Should I give one more team a try before hanging up my cleats? Should I quit my job and pursue my calling full-time? Do I have what it takes to make it in this field?*—there will never be a shortage of opinions and advice. Some will be good, and some will be bad, hence the need to choose your counselors wisely. And even if you stumble momentarily, when you commit yourself to fulfilling the purpose God has assigned you, He will remain faithful.

So seek wise counsel. Consider the source. Spend time centering yourself in prayer and meditating on Scripture. And heed the wisdom of the apostle Paul: "Don't worry about anything; instead, pray about everything. Tell God what you need, and thank him for all he has done. Then you will experience God's peace, which exceeds anything we can understand" (Philippians 4:6-7).

DEVELOPING YOUR GAME PLAN

1. How do you react to my story about being confronted by an agent who assumed he knew what was best for me and my career? If you've had an experience when someone gave you advice that conflicted with what

you felt you should be doing, how did you respond? How has positive advice impacted your life?

2. How can we determine whether the advice we're getting is good or bad? What are some qualities we should look for in our "counselors"? What are some ways we can seek counsel from God?

3. What can we learn from the life of Samson? How did he succeed and fail in his calling as a leader of Israel? What role did wise counsel (or the lack of it) play in his life?

4. Who are a few people in your life right now that you could consider "counselors"? They might be family members, friends, mentors, or coworkers. Tell them about your journey to try to discover your calling, and ask them if they are willing to talk with you and give insight into some decisions you are considering.

Chapter 4
NOTHING IS WASTED

MAKE THE MOST OF
EVERY OPPORTUNITY

Every August, NFL teams must trim their active rosters from ninety players down to just fifty-three. It is a huge drop, one that leaves more than a thousand young hopefuls out on the street, looking for a job. It's known as Roster Cut Down Day, and it is twenty-four hours of sheer torture.

My clients and I spend the entire day staring at our phones, praying they don't ring. You see, teams only call the players they've decided to waive, so for most players, silence in August is golden.

It's hard to describe the devastation that accompanies those calls. Most of these guys have never been cut from anything before. They have always been the best of the best.

Then, all of a sudden, someone is telling them they aren't good enough, and it . . . is . . . *brutal*.

One Roster Cut Down Day was especially difficult. It was 2009, and after four drafts as a certified NFL agent, I was still trying to sign my first drafted client and waiting to see if one of my undrafted players, a young fullback named James who had been picked up as a free agent, would make the Cowboys' final fifty-three-man roster.

I was attending a kickoff party for the first OU game of the season when my cell phone rang. As soon as I saw the area code, my heart sank. I quickly ducked down the hall, away from the celebration.

"Hello, this is Kelli," I said, steeling myself for the worst.

"Hi, Kelli." I recognized the voice instantly. It was Todd Williams, director of football operations for the Cowboys. "I'm so sorry," he said, "but James didn't make the cut. We are releasing him today, and we don't see a need for him on our practice squad."

His words hit me like a load of bricks. Choking back tears, I muttered, "I understand. Thanks, Todd." As I clicked "End Call," my emotions overwhelmed me, and I sat down on the floor and wept. For years, I had poured everything I had into building an agency and recruiting clients. And here I was four years later with absolutely nothing to show for it. None of my clients had made it to an NFL regular season roster. I'd received zero compensation for all the hours I'd invested. (Practice squad players get paid; their agents do not. We only get paid when they make the final fifty-three-man roster.) And without a proven track record as an agent, I was afraid it would become even more difficult for me to attract new clients who were likely to be successful.

Then my thoughts turned to James, who had also poured everything he had into pursuing his dream. *Poor James.* Barring an unexpected serendipity, such as another player getting hurt at the last minute, the Cowboys' decision not to offer him a spot on their practice squad pretty much signaled the end of the road with this team.

> *Don't give up. Stay focused. Learn from this. Your time will come.*

Resigned, I scrolled down to James's name on my phone, wiped the tears from my cheeks, and took a deep, cleansing breath. But for some reason, I couldn't bring myself to hit "Call." I stared at the screen so long that it eventually went black, leaving me face-to-face with my own tearstained reflection. I pinched the bridge of my nose and tried to think of something positive to say. *Don't give up. Stay focused. Learn from this. Your time will come.*

Suddenly, my mind flashed back ten years to the last time I'd found myself sitting on the floor in tears . . . thinking this exact same thing.

THE PLEASURES PRINCIPLE

It was December of 1998, and I was in my third year of law school. The year before, I had competed in and won the Miss Oklahoma pageant. In addition to being a wonderful experience, it also provided enough scholarship money to pay for the remainder of my law school education. After taking a year off to travel around Oklahoma and the rest of the country, speaking and doing special appearances, I returned to law school to find that all of the paid legal internships had already been snapped up by my classmates. That left me with only one other viable option for a job that would cover my living expenses: the mall.

As it happened, a friend of mine from church was in charge of the Estée Lauder counter at Dillard's department store, and she offered me a job selling cosmetics. The hours were flexible, and the pay was decent, but it felt as though I had just taken a giant step backward. Not only was I not doing anything even remotely connected to the legal profession, but after a year of having a team of people take care of my hair, makeup, and wardrobe, here I was hawking blush, perfume, and moisturizer at the local mall, of all places. It was humbling and, to be perfectly honest, a little embarrassing. And then it got worse.

That season, Estée Lauder launched a new men's cologne to accompany their bestselling women's perfume, Pleasures. It was called Pleasures for Men, and part of my first week on the job was spent walking through the store and handing out samples while wearing an apron with the cologne's name and logo on it. That's right, I was the official Pleasures for Men girl—and I hated it. I had no sales experience, and it didn't take me long to realize that trying to push products on people who clearly weren't interested was not in my DNA.

After a few days, my boss moved me back behind the makeup counter, but I was still struggling.

I remember watching the other saleswomen upsell merchandise and push customers toward one product or the other—sometimes both. At first it really bothered me. One woman in particular seemed to excel at getting customers to buy more than they came in for. If someone came in wanting powder, she would say, "You can't use this powder without this foundation." If they came in to buy lipstick, she would tell them, "You can't wear this lipstick without this lip liner." She didn't even seem to listen when they told her they weren't interested. In fact, I suspect that a lot of her customers bought whatever she suggested just to get away from her.

Is this what it takes to be in sales? I wondered. *Because if it is, I am* not *going to make it here.* Needless to say, my first few weeks on the job were miserable. Every day, I came to work feeling embarrassed, underutilized, and utterly convinced I was wasting my time. Then one day, I was sitting on the floor of the storage room, stocking inventory, and the tears just started flowing. *What am I doing here? I was Miss Oklahoma. I competed in the Miss America pageant. And now I'm doing free makeovers for high school girls who have no intention of buying anything?* I wasn't using the skills I'd gained as Miss Oklahoma, I wasn't using my journalism degree or law school education or learning what it was like to be a practicing attorney, and I wasn't even doing something I was good at. I felt as though I had hit rock bottom. That's when I realized there was nowhere to go but up.

Okay, I reasoned, *if I'm going to be here, I'm going to gain something from it.* I knew my classmates were likely learning valuable skills clerking at law firms. The question was: What could I learn from selling makeup?

I started watching the other sales ladies like a hawk. While the pushy clerk still made me uncomfortable, I noticed another saleswoman who took a decidedly different approach. Instead of doing a hard sell, she actually engaged with her customers, asked them questions about their preferences, and then made recommendations based on their answers. She complimented them and made them feel beautiful.

"Your eyes are so pretty," she would say. "I really love this color on you." And it wasn't a sales job. She genuinely took an interest in people, talking with them about their jobs and their kids while she did their makeup. She made them feel valued.

I also noticed that her customers spent just as much if not more money with her as they did with the pushy woman. The difference was her clients actually came back! Whenever a special promotion came up, she would pull out a book with dozens of her clients' names and numbers in it, call them up, and let them know about the sale. More often than not, her investment paid off.

Both women had strong sales. But while one had one-time customers, the other had long-term clients. While one was making transactions, the other was building relationships—and *that* was something I could see myself doing.

As I started modeling my sales technique after the second

clerk, I was surprised to discover how much I suddenly enjoyed the job. I loved making a connection with someone, helping her feel more valued and more beautiful than she did when we met, and really investing in her as a person. Over the next several weeks, I went from having a genuine disdain for sales to learning how to identify people's needs and find workable solutions for them. And in the process, I developed negotiation, listening, and people skills that I still use today.

My entire business model is relational. I'm not trying to force a player into a system he won't fit into or saddle a team with a player they don't really want or need just to collect a check. I'm developing long-term relationships with the goal of helping multiple parties find win-win solutions. My approach is: "Your team has a particular need. I have a client I believe will fill that need. Let's talk about how we can make this work for everyone."

Who would have thought you could learn so much about being a sports agent from working at a cosmetics counter?

Once again, God knew exactly what He was doing when He set me on this path. What I initially saw as a waste of time and a step backward, He saw as a training ground that would help me develop the skills I would need to be successful down the road. With God, nothing is wasted. I believe that every experience we have, we have for a reason. Our role isn't to question it or complain about it but rather to embrace it and then learn everything we can. Our role is to tell ourselves, *Don't give up. Stay focused. Learn from this. Your time will come.*

Unfortunately, James, my fullback who was cut by the Cowboys, opted not to follow that wisdom. When I gave him the news, I offered to try to find him a spot on another team's practice squad in hopes that he might catch on somewhere, but he wasn't interested. In his mind, it was "go big or go home," and when big didn't happen right away, he packed up and went. A few years later, however, I had another client who, like the Estée Lauder rep I came to admire, had a decidedly different attitude.

PERSEVERANCE PAYS OFF

I met tight end Blake Jarwin in 2016. A tall, somewhat lanky kid with dreams of playing big-time football, Blake had a quiet confidence that I admired instantly. There was no arrogance or pridefulness about him, just a fierce determination to be excellent in everything he did. After we solidified a friendship based on shared values and mutual respect, it was my honor to sign him as a client for the 2017 NFL Draft.

That spring, Blake was passed over for the Combine, which all of the top players hope to be invited to. If he was disappointed, he never showed it. He simply put his head down and went to work, determined to be his best.

When the draft finally arrived, we knew, based on the process leading up to that moment, there was a possibility that Blake would be drafted; but we were prepared in the event that he wasn't.

For those who are unfamiliar with the draft and what happens immediately afterward, let me paint the picture. A player and his family and friends sit through three painfully long days, watching the procedure on TV and waiting for a team to call and say, "We're going to make you a Cowboy [Seahawk, Raider, etc.]!" As they endure seven rounds of name after name being announced, pre-draft excitement gives way to frustration, confusion, anger, and finally—as the last player (who is literally dubbed "Mr. Irrelevant") is announced—hopelessness. Yet for most players, that's when the real excitement begins.

While each team selects approximately seven players in the draft (some more, some less based on trades, compensatory picks, and other mechanisms), they still have to fill out their ninety-man rosters by signing even more rookies immediately after the draft. These players get three-year contracts instead of the four-year deals given to draft picks, and their signing bonuses are typically a fraction of the drafted players'. However, they do get the opportunity to compete for a roster spot alongside draft picks. This is what is known as college free agency, and it is absolutely chaotic. Teams rapidly contact all the players they considered draftable who did not get picked up, and they work these lists so fast that deals often get done within minutes.

As the final draft picks were made, and Blake's name still hadn't been announced, I called him from my office/war room and said, "Here we go. I'll bring you the free agency offers and make recommendations, but the final decision is yours. Be ready. It's going to come at you fast."

Blake *was* ready. He was calm. Calls started coming. Every

team on our pre-draft top-five list called to sign him, and by the end of the night, Blake had signed with the Dallas Cowboys.

Blake's first training camp with the Cowboys was eye-opening for him. He learned the Cowboys' offense right alongside one of the best to ever play the tight end position, Jason Witten. But at the end of preseason, when the Cowboys trimmed their roster to fifty-three players, Blake did not make the initial cut. The team did, however, offer him a spot on their practice squad.

Practice squad members endure the same grueling practices as members of the active roster. They shoulder all the same obligations, but they don't receive either the pay or the glory that players on the active roster do. (In fact, the practice squad used to be called the "taxi squad" because players had to provide their own transportation to and from games.) And when it comes time to actually play the game, practice squad members don't get to suit up and often watch from home or from the stands just like the rest of us.

Most players consider the practice squad a consolation prize. Technically you're part of the team, but it's definitely not the spot you were hoping for. A lot of players in James's position consider it a step-down—the NFL equivalent of working at a cosmetics counter when you're hoping for a legal internship.

Blake could have looked at it that way and slacked off or just plain given up, but instead, he embraced the opportunity. He never complained or felt sorry for himself. He remained focused and went to work every single day, learning everything he could and constantly looking for ways to improve. And his persistence paid off. Several weeks into that 2017 season, the Cowboys signed Blake to the active roster. He has since gone on to experience a level of success, including several clutch plays during the 2019 Divisional Playoffs, that has surprised many in the league. And he's just getting started.

Blake stayed faithful to his calling and made the best of what many would consider an undesirable situation. He didn't view playing on the practice squad as a waste of his time and talent because he knew that it wasn't. From day one, he saw it as an opportunity to learn, to improve, and to prove to both himself and others that he has what it takes to reach his ultimate goal.

And that has made all the difference.

THE ONCE AND FUTURE KING

It's one thing to set your sights on playing on Monday Night Football only to end up working your tail off in anonymity on the practice squad. But imagine being anointed the king of Israel—chosen by God Himself, no less—only to spend the next several years serving as a lowly shepherd and a court musician! That's exactly what happened to David.

David was the youngest of eight sons born in Bethlehem to a man named Jesse. One day, God sent His prophet, Samuel, to Jesse's home, telling him, "I have selected one of his sons to be my king" (1 Samuel 16:1).

When Samuel arrived, Jesse introduced him to his sons one

by one, beginning with the oldest. When Samuel saw Eliab, the eldest son, he "thought, 'Surely this is the LORD's anointed!' But the LORD said to Samuel, 'Don't judge by his appearance or height, for I have rejected him. The LORD doesn't see things the way you see them. People judge by outward appearance, but the LORD looks at the heart'" (verses 6-7).

After Jesse introduced his first seven sons to Samuel—all of whom God rejected—Samuel said, "Are these all the sons you have?" Jesse replied, "There is still the youngest, but he's out in the fields watching the sheep and goats" (verse 11).

Even David's own father was about to pass him over! Talk about Mr. Irrelevant.

"Send for him at once," Samuel said. "We will not sit down to eat until he arrives" (verse 11).

So Jesse sent for David. And as soon as David entered the room, Samuel knew. *This* was the future king of Israel.

"This is the one," the Lord confirmed. "Anoint him" (verse 12).

In that moment, Samuel anointed David with oil in front of all his brothers. Through Samuel, God called David to be king.

But David did not immediately ascend to the throne. In fact, many years would pass before David would be recognized as the rightful king. Instead, immediately after Samuel anointed him, David returned to tending his father's sheep out in the fields. Think about that! Moments after being anointed the future king of Israel, David went right back to his job as a lowly shepherd. But that's not all.

When the current king, Saul, became depressed, David, who was a skillful musician, was summoned to the palace to entertain him by playing the harp. Now, David could have fussed, whined, or complained about serving the king rather than being installed as king himself, but instead, he played so well that Saul took a liking to him and asked David to stay on full-time as his official armor bearer. He did, traveling back and forth between the king's court and his father's fields.

Now, it may seem as though David was being asked to punch well below his weight, working not just one but two jobs—neither of which seemed to be getting him any closer to his calling. But as usual, God knew exactly what He was doing.

You see, David was anointed when he was still very young, only a teenager. So, while he may have been destined for greatness, he still had a lot to learn. By putting him in close proximity to King Saul, God made it possible for David to observe the king and learn the ins and outs of leading a nation. As for the shepherding? There was a method to God's madness there as well.

Shortly after David had entered Saul's service, the Israelites found themselves on the brink of war against their old enemies the Philistines. When a colossal nine-foot-tall Philistine soldier named Goliath challenged any of the Israelites to fight him one-on-one, none of the men in Saul's army felt capable enough to take him on—except one.

"Don't worry about this Philistine," David told Saul. "I'll go fight him!"

"Don't be ridiculous!" Saul replied. "There's no way you can fight this Philistine and possibly win! You're only a boy, and he's been a man of war since his youth."

But David persisted. "I have been taking care of my father's sheep and goats," he said. "When a lion or a bear comes to steal a lamb from the flock, I go after it with a club and rescue the lamb from its mouth. If the animal turns on me, I catch it by the jaw and club it to death. I have done this to both lions and bears, and I'll do it to this pagan Philistine, too, for he has defied the armies of the living God! The LORD who rescued me from the claws of the lion and the bear will rescue me from this Philistine!"

I SAMUEL 17:32-37

Not only did David take on Goliath; he conquered him. (More on this later.) And this feat would not have been possible had David not honed his skills guarding the flocks out in the fields. God had been carefully preparing David for the day he would gain a place of power and influence. When the time came, David was ready to step up because he had remained faithful in the daily tasks that would eventually lead him to his God-given destiny.

THE ULTIMATE DREAM JOB

Another excellent example of someone making the most of a less-than-desirable situation is Joseph. Like David, Joseph was the youngest of a large family of brothers (eleven!). And like David, Joseph worked in the fields, tending his father's flocks.

When Joseph was just seventeen, God gave him a dream. "Listen to this dream," Joseph said to his brothers. "We were out in the field, tying up bundles of grain. Suddenly my bundle stood up, and your bundles all gathered around and bowed low before mine!" (Genesis 37:6-7). Needless to say, his brothers were not happy with the symbolism. Nor were they pleased when Joseph told them about another dream God had given him, in which "the sun, moon, and eleven stars bowed low before" him (verse 9). In fact, the brothers were so angry with Joseph for implying not once, but twice, that they would one day bow down to him, that they threw him in a pit and later sold him into slavery. Talk about sibling rivalry!

Eventually, Joseph was sold to Potiphar, captain of the palace guards in Egypt. Once again, this seems like a pretty significant step-down for someone whose dreams suggested he was called to greatness. Yet, instead of bemoaning his fate, Joseph worked hard every day. Potiphar was so impressed with Joseph's work ethic that he promoted him, placing "him in charge of his entire household and everything he owned" (Genesis 39:4).

Unfortunately, Potiphar's wife also took a liking to Joseph. When Joseph remained loyal to his master and refused her advances, she lied to her husband, telling him Joseph had attacked her. Potiphar was so upset, he had Joseph thrown in jail.

Despite getting knocked down yet again, Joseph didn't throw in the towel or complain. Instead, he held fast to his belief that God had a greater purpose for him someday. In the meantime, he used his God-given talent of interpreting dreams to win the favor of Pharaoh. When Joseph predicted a massive famine and explained how Pharaoh could stockpile enough food beforehand to keep his people alive, Pharaoh rewarded Joseph by placing him in charge of all of Egypt, proclaiming, "You will be in charge of my court, and all my people will take orders from you. Only I, sitting on my throne, will have a rank higher than yours. . . . I am Pharaoh, but no one will lift a hand or foot in the entire land of Egypt without your approval" (Genesis 41:40, 44).

Years later, starving and desperate during the long famine that extended even to their homeland, Joseph's brothers went to Egypt to purchase food. When they approached Joseph with their request, they didn't even recognize him at first—and they bowed to the ground in front of him, fulfilling the prophecy that God had revealed to Joseph in his dreams years before.

First slavery, then prison. It would have been so easy for Joseph to write his situation off as hopeless. Yet in each instance, he trusted God's plan for him, worked hard, and made the most of his God-given talents. And in each instance, his diligence and positive attitude were rewarded.

YOU REAP WHAT YOU SOW

The apostle Paul wrote that we should "not grow weary while doing good, for in due season we shall reap if we do not lose heart" (Galatians 6:9, NKJV)—advice that carries even more weight because Paul wrote it while in prison.

As you pursue your calling, things may not always go as planned. Sometimes taking a step forward requires taking a step sideways or backward. The way you respond to these "missteps" can mean the difference between fulfilling your calling and abandoning it.

The way you respond to these "missteps" can mean the difference between fulfilling your calling and abandoning it.

Remember, when God puts you on the path, He doesn't guarantee that it's going to be straight, easy, or even pleasant. But more often than not, those twists and turns, stops and starts, are what prepare us for what's coming next; teach us about who we are and what we're capable of; and reveal God's will for our lives. Remaining faithful to our calling is not a matter of simply being patient and waiting for rough patches to pass. It's an attitude. A mindset. A determination to stay the course no matter what circumstances or delays we might face.

When things don't go as planned, work hard and persevere. When you get knocked down, get back up! See your circumstances as an opportunity to grow and make progress. Maintaining a commitment to pursue your calling doesn't mean that you will always succeed, but it will ensure that you keep moving forward. By staying faithful in the small things. By practicing daily discipline. By being excellent right where you are and making the most of every situation.

Blake Jarwin could have given up when he didn't make the Cowboys' final roster right off the bat. King David could have grown discouraged when he was sent back out to the fields after being anointed the future king of Israel. Joseph could have accepted defeat after being sold into slavery or thrown in prison. But each of these young men stayed committed to his calling and chose to make the most of his situation. And look what God did!

That same choice belongs to each of us. Remember, God doesn't waste anything. Every challenge, every setback, every encounter He places in our paths is there for a reason. *Don't give up. Stay focused. Learn from this. Your time will come.*

DEVELOPING YOUR GAME PLAN

1. What was a time you were asked to do a task that you weren't good at or that didn't seem worthwhile? Even if you didn't think you learned from it at the time, can you look back now and see some ways you benefited from the experience?

2. If we believe that God is using circumstances in our lives to help us grow, is it valid to consider any task "beneath us"? How can we be patient and receptive when we feel that what we're doing isn't getting us any closer to fulfilling our callings?

3. What does it mean to you that with God in charge of our lives, nothing is wasted? How can God use our

setbacks to shape us? How do the stories of Joseph and David encourage you as you think about this concept?

4. What's one less-than-ideal situation in your life right now where you can challenge yourself to work hard and learn? Write down some skills or abilities you might be able to develop through this experience, and consider how they could fit in with what you think God is calling you to do. How could a better attitude help you view this challenge as an opportunity?

Chapter 5

THE GIFT OF FAILURE

LEARN FROM YOUR MISTAKES

When I first became an agent, I had no idea how to recruit new clients, and I mean *none*. I figured that if I developed enough connections in football, the scouts and coaches I got to know would inform me about all the best prospects, tell them how wonderful *I* was, and then help us connect with one another. Surprisingly, that's not *quite* how it works.

Regardless, shortly after I got my certification, I reached out to a handful of coaches and scouts, told them I'd just passed my agent exam, and asked them if they knew of anyone I should be keeping an eye on that season. Two of them mentioned a specific offensive lineman at OU, whom they'd been tracking for several seasons.

"He could be a first-rounder this spring," they said.

I thought, *Awesome! I'd love to sign a first-round draft pick right out of the gate!*

That season I went to every OU game, both home and away, to watch this player. That's when it struck me: I had no idea what I was looking for. I'd been a football fan my entire life, but while certain players—like quarterbacks, running backs, or wide receivers—naturally stood out, I didn't have the slightest idea what a good offensive or defensive lineman looked like.

I also had no idea how to get in front of this young man. I asked anyone I could think of if they had his contact information, but they either didn't have it or didn't want to hand it over to some newbie agent.

As it happens, that season OU earned a bid to play the Oregon Ducks in the Holiday Bowl. Realizing I was running out of time to finally meet this young man before the season ended, I decided to attend. The day of the game, I went to the hotel lobby, where the players and their families were waiting for buses to take them over to the stadium. I did a quick scan of the room and saw my potential client sitting on a sofa with his girlfriend.

I wasn't sure how much time I had, so I quickly made my way over to him, rehearsing my spiel as I wove through the crowd. *Hello, my name is Kelli Masters and I'm an agent. I've been watching you all season, and I'd like to speak with you. Hello, my name is Kelli Masters and I'm an agent. I've been following your career, and I'd like to talk with you about your future. Hello, I'm Kelli Masters . . .*

When I arrived at the couch, the young man was completely engrossed in his phone, so I cleared my throat to get his attention. Both he and his girlfriend looked up at me, and I promptly froze solid. I blinked a couple times, then I stuck my hand out and said, "Hi, I'm Kelli. I'm an agent. I would love to represent you! Can I give you my number?" Smooth, huh?

Needless to say, they looked at me like I was nuts. And frankly, I couldn't blame them.

"Yeah, thanks," the player said, stifling a laugh. "We already know what we're doing." And with that, he went right back to his phone.

"Okay . . . ," I stammered, slowly backing away. "Thanks. Have a nice day." *Good Lord.*

Talk about mortifying. I didn't even go to the game. I just slunk back to my room and prayed that nobody else in the lobby had seen me make a complete idiot out of myself—and that if and when the player told the story to his friends later that night, he would forget my name. A few months later, he was drafted in the second round and went on to play in the NFL for eleven years.

That was 2006, which you may recall was the year I told off one of the industry's premier agents for having the audacity to suggest that I didn't know what I was doing. Who are we kidding? In many respects, he was right. I *didn't* know what I was doing—*yet.* But then, people who are just starting out in a new field rarely do. That's why they call them "rookie mistakes." It takes time, experience, and a lot of adjustments to master a new skill. And yes, sometimes those early mistakes can be costly. This one potentially cost me a second-round client. But as these words often attributed to Winston Churchill remind us, "Success is not final, failure is not fatal: it is the courage to continue that counts."

Every mistake we make—every failure we experience—provides us with an opportunity to learn, to grow, and to improve.

Failure is only fatal if you let it be. In my years as an agent, I have tried to consider failure to be a gift. Why? Because every mistake we make—every failure we experience—provides us with an opportunity to learn, to grow, and to improve.

I made a lot of mistakes my first season as an agent, but the biggest by far was not doing my homework. I had faith that I had found my true calling, and I believed I had what it took to make it in this industry. But blind faith and belief weren't enough. I walked into that hotel lobby completely unprepared. It wouldn't happen again.

IF AT FIRST . . .

After the Holiday Bowl fiasco, I took stock of everything I'd learned (i.e., done wrong). First, I realized being a lifelong fan with a decent but basic understanding of football wasn't good enough. I needed to educate myself on exactly what it was NFL scouts and teams were looking for. In other words, I needed to know what separated a highly graded running back, offensive lineman, or defensive end from one who was considered by scouts to be a likely free agent—or worse, unlikely to be picked up by the NFL at all.

So, that off-season, I spent a lot of time talking with scouts and coaches, picking their brains on what makes a great player. I didn't even try to put up a front. I asked, "What is it about so-and-so that you like so much?" "What did you see in his film that made you grade him the way you did?" "What are you looking for in the pre-draft evaluation process?"

Though everyone had a slightly different take, certain key characteristics came up time and time again. Things like athleticism, quickness, motor skills, ability to read the field, and vision. But what did all of *that* mean? I still had more to learn.

At a get-together with friends, I asked one of them, Chris Stiles, who had spent years coaching high school football, to teach me what I needed to know. As he began explaining what the different positions did, I stopped him and said, "I need you to *show* me." We walked to a more open area of the room we were all gathered in and I said, "Okay, so if I'm standing here and I'm a middle linebacker, what's my role? What should I be doing?"

We went through each position, with Chris walking me through what every player needed to do before and after the ball is snapped, during a run play or a passing play, when special teams are employed, and so forth—all so I would know what to look for in potential recruits.

That summer I watched hours of old games, zeroing in on specific positions, taking voracious notes, and comparing players to what Chris and all the coaches and scouts had told me. It took time, but eventually it started to make sense. I started to see it.

As I learned more about football, I also learned about agent protocol. I figured out that there is a right time and a wrong time to introduce yourself to a prospective client. Hours before a high-stakes Bowl Game, in the hotel lobby, when the player is surrounded by family and friends and waiting for the team bus to take him to the stadium? That would be the wrong time.

I've since learned that the best time to approach new clients is early on in their freshman or sophomore year, when they are still open-minded and learning about the recruiting process themselves. That way I have a chance not only to introduce myself but also to educate them on what's coming down the line and to create a customized plan for moving forward. Making contact that early also gives me a chance to get to know and interact with the players' parents, who can obviously be influential when it comes to making major career decisions.

I create what I used to call a "trial notebook," similar to what I put together when I was an attorney preparing for a case. In it I include everything I know about a player, such as his full bio, statistical information, career highlights, strengths, weaknesses, and injuries. I also include what round comparable players were drafted in the previous three years plus sample contracts for similar players. I create a personalized write-up for each player that includes a detailed explanation of the services I provide leading up to, during, and after the draft, as well as a full career and post-career legacy plan.

Over the years, I have refined and improved upon the process. While I haven't signed every client I've pursued, I can assure you my current approach has proven far more effective than "Hi, I'm Kelli. Can I give you my number?"

In fact, just five years after my Holiday Bowl humiliation, one of my clients was selected number three overall in the 2010 Draft (a story I'll talk more about in chapter 7). And it never would have happened if I hadn't failed first.

DO YOUR HOMEWORK

Whenever you start a new venture (or adventure), it's a challenge not to let your enthusiasm get the better of you. Don't get me wrong, enthusiasm and excitement are wonderful things! But like anything else, they need to be channeled properly. Rushing in blindly without any kind of plan will almost always yield bad results. Take your time. Do your homework. Talk to other people in your field of interest. Ask them what they've learned over the years—what they wish they'd known going in, or what they'd do differently now, and why. You might be able to benefit from some of *their* mistakes before they become your own.

It may sound like a cliché, but knowledge really is power. Investing time up front to learn your craft is never wasted.

How can you expect to do anything well if you don't take the time to learn about it first?

Before my clients enter free agency, I always sit down with them and ask not where they *want* to play if given the chance, but where they feel they can be most successful. Everyone has a dream team—somewhere they'd love to play because they like the location or have an affinity for the team. But dreams are one thing; reality is another. That's why my clients and I talk about the different coaching staffs, the types of offense or defense each team runs, and how my players would factor into that. We look at the rest of each team's roster to get an idea of what their competition will look like. Do they want to be a starter right away, or would they be content to play a backup role for a season or two? And then there are the non-football questions. Would they be happy living in a big metropolitan area like New York or Los Angeles, or would they rather be in a smaller market like Tampa or Green Bay? What are the taxes like in each location? How much do they stand to make in salary? How much would they need to live on? Do they have a family to consider? If they have kids, where would they be happiest?

I want my clients to weigh *all* the options and think about what's in their best interest for the long haul. They may not always make the right choice, but I try to give them every opportunity to make an informed decision.

Doing your homework is one of the best ways to avoid rookie mistakes. But even so, mistakes are inevitable. If you're going to make one, let it be *your* mistake. Own it. And then, after the initial sting wears off, learn from it, and let that learning inform your decisions moving forward.

TRUST YOUR GUT

A few years back, I received a call from a friend who was an alum of a major university asking me if I would be willing to take on a particular player from that school as a client. I did a little preliminary research and discovered that while this young man was an extremely talented player, he'd also had some significant run-ins with the law during his college days, which is almost always a red flag during the draft. So I thanked my friend for thinking of me, and I politely declined.

Two years later, the alum reached out to me again. It turns out the player had gotten picked up by an NFL team, put in a few months on their practice squad, and was then signed by a different team to their active roster.

"So what do you need me for?" I asked.

Apparently the alum, who had taken on this player as a special project, felt his current agent wasn't doing everything he could to ensure this young man's long-term success in the league. He felt my "more nurturing approach" would be a better fit.

Hesitant but flattered, I agreed to meet with the player in person. He was very charming. He assured me that he'd turned over a new leaf and said he wanted to do things right for a change.

Frankly, I was torn. On the one hand, I really didn't want to get involved with a player who had a criminal record. I'd been around the league long enough to see the impact that pressure, fame, and sudden financial freedom can have on players with already "shaky" histories, and it rarely turns out well. On the other hand, the more idealistic part of me wondered if players like this weren't the reason I'd become an agent in the first place. I wanted to be a mentor. He needed a mentor. I wanted to help guide young athletes through their careers, and this young man clearly needed guidance. It seemed like a perfect fit—*right?*

Still, just to be safe, I put in a call to a friend of mine who was an attorney in this player's hometown and asked his opinion. He told me, "He's a good kid, but be careful; he'll tell you what you want to hear."

I thought back to our first meeting. This young man seemed genuine about his change of heart. And even if he wasn't, I could handle it—*right?*

Despite a check in my gut, I agreed to sign the player at the end of the regular season. The problems started almost immediately. First came the criminal allegations. Then the drugs. Then more problems with the law. I tried for months to get him to straighten out his life. I worked with the NFL, his team, everyone I could think of to get him back on track. Then one night, about midway through the season, my phone rang. It was 3 a.m. I recognized the number.

Great, I thought. *He's probably in jail and needs someone to bail him out.*

It was him, all right. But he wasn't calling to ask for bail money. He was calling to fire me.

"What?!" I blurted out. *After everything I've done to salvage your rapidly disintegrating career,* this *is the thanks I get?*

That's when things took an even more bizarre twist. It turned out another agent had offered this guy two hundred thousand dollars to sign with him, so my client's plan was to fire me, sign with the other guy, get the money—and then fire him and come back to me.

"You can't do that," I told him. "It's illegal and completely unethical." But he didn't listen. He never did.

After he fired me, I simply refused to take him back. The truth is I never should have taken him on as a client in the first place. And as much as I would love to pin that call on someone else, in the end, the decision was all mine.

My gut told me taking on this player was a bad idea. I should have heeded that instinct. My attorney friend told me this guy was trouble. I should have listened to him. In fact, his comments should have triggered me to dig a little deeper—to speak to the player's old coaches, guidance counselors, and teammates to see if they'd had the same experience. I should have done a lot of things differently.

And yet, despite all the lost time and energy I poured into my client that season, the experience helped me become a better agent. It taught me to trust my gut and to always—always—do my research before taking on a "questionable" client.

As painful as our personal failures can be, they are also our greatest teachers, driving lessons home in ways that lectures and admonishments simply can't. And often, we come out on the other side stronger, more committed, and better equipped to take on challenges than ever before.

THIRD TIME'S A CHARM

If you need further proof that failure isn't fatal, consider the story of Peter, who was one of the twelve disciples chosen by Jesus to bear witness to His ministry and help spread His message on earth. But even though Peter was a devoted disciple, he was also a deeply flawed human being who often let his emotions get the best of him.

The Gospels tell us that Peter worked as a fisherman, but he was hardly what you would call a quiet, solitary figure. Outspoken, rash, and impetuous, Peter frequently challenged Jesus and was actually scolded by Him multiple times: first for trying, along with the other disciples, to shoo children away from him while he was preaching (see Mark 10:13-15), again for not allowing Jesus to wash his feet (see John 13:3-8), a third time for falling asleep in the garden of Gethsemane while Jesus prayed (see Matthew 26:40-41), and then finally for rashly cutting off a soldier's ear during Jesus' arrest (see John 18:10-11). Jesus even called Peter Satan at one point when Peter suggested that Jesus didn't really need to die: "Get away from me, Satan! You are a dangerous trap to me. You are seeing things merely from a human point of view, not from God's" (Matthew 16:23).

And of course, there was the time when Peter tried to walk on water:

Shortly before dawn Jesus went out to them, walking on the lake. When the disciples saw him walking on the lake, they were terrified. "It's a ghost," they said, and cried out in fear.

But Jesus immediately said to them: "Take courage! It is I. Don't be afraid."

"Lord, if it's you," Peter replied, "tell me to come to you on the water."

"Come," he said.

Then Peter got down out of the boat, walked on the water and came toward Jesus. But when he saw the wind, he was afraid and, beginning to sink, cried out, "Lord, save me!"

Immediately Jesus reached out his hand and caught him. "You of little faith," he said, "why did you doubt?"

MATTHEW 14:25-31, NIV

Now, I'm not going to call this an unqualified failure. Peter did get out of the boat and actually walked on water momentarily, which is more than any of the other disciples did. But just when things were going well—right when he was experiencing an actual miracle—he let fear overwhelm him, and he started to sink. Not his best moment.

But without question, Peter's biggest—and most infamous—misstep was when he denied knowing Jesus not once, not twice, but *three* times on the eve of the Crucifixion. The last time, his denial was vehement: "Man, I don't know what you are talking about" (Luke 22:60). Mind you, this is *after* Jesus had already healed Peter's mother-in-law, performed a plethora of miracles, and predicted His own arrest, death, and resurrection—*in Peter's presence*!

Peter was one of the first disciples Jesus recruited and was one of His closest friends and confidants. And yet, time and time again, when the chips were down, Peter let Jesus down.

Now, you would think that after all of that, Jesus would simply wash His hands of Peter and move on to a more reliable guy to help with His ministry. But that's the beautiful thing about Jesus and failure: As long as you genuinely believe in one (Jesus), the other (failure) is impossible.

Despite his flaws, Peter did believe in Jesus, wholly and completely. So, shortly after the Resurrection, Jesus gave Peter the opportunity to redeem himself, asking him three times, "Do you love me?" Each time, Peter responded with "You know I love you." And after each of Peter's responses, Jesus responded, "Then feed my sheep" (John 21:17). By giving Peter an instruction to love and teach and guide others seeking truth, Jesus gave Peter his calling.

Before Jesus even met Peter, He knew how their relationship would play out. He knew Peter struggled to control his emotions. He knew Peter was impetuous and often spoke out of turn. And He knew that when tensions boiled over before the trial and Crucifixion, Peter would, out of fear, deny knowing Him three times. And yet, despite all his weaknesses and failures, Peter listened to Jesus, and the revelation he received became the bedrock of the church. Jesus told him,

Now I say to you that you are Peter (which means
"rock"), and upon this rock I will build my church,
and all the powers of hell will not conquer it. And
I will give you the keys of the Kingdom of Heaven.
Whatever you forbid on earth will be forbidden in
heaven, and whatever you permit on earth will be
permitted in heaven.
MATTHEW 16:18-19

Peter went on to become a great leader in the early
church, sharing Jesus' message of love and hope and con-
verting thousands of men and women to Christianity. His
failures were not fatal. They helped him develop the kind
of character and resolve Jesus knew he would need to start
the church.

As Romans 5:3-5 says, "We can rejoice, too, when we
run into problems and trials, for we know that they help
us develop endurance. And endurance develops strength of
character, and character strengthens our confident hope of
salvation. And this hope will not lead to disappointment."

FAILURE IS NOT FATAL

We all make mistakes, but our failures are not the end of us.
Failure only becomes final when we refuse to learn from it.
So when things go wrong—and they will—don't let it get
you down. Let it make you even better, smarter, and more
determined than you were before.

Remember, God doesn't waste anything. Just like Jesus

did for Peter, He has put you on the path you're on knowing full well the challenges, letdowns, and missteps you'll endure along the way. But those challenges and missteps are there for a reason—not to get in the way of you achieving your goals but to show you *how* to achieve them. Every failure you endure, every misstep you recover from is one more weapon in your arsenal—one more "Look what I know how to do now" and one more "Well . . . I won't let *that* happen again."

> *Failure only becomes final when we refuse to learn from it.*

If things had always gone right for me, I would not be as strong or as resilient as I am now. If I'd never had any problems to fix, I wouldn't know how to fix things. If everything had always been smooth sailing, I would never have learned what *doesn't* work. The road toward my calling hasn't always been easy, but I can promise you it's been worth it. And it will be for you, too.

Remember, failures aren't there to taunt us or to prove to us that we *can't*. They're there to teach us and to strengthen us so that someday we *can*.

DEVELOPING YOUR GAME PLAN

1. As you look back over your life, what are some lessons that you wouldn't have learned without an experience of failure? How did failure serve as a catalyst to help you learn and change?

2. In the story about my "problem" client, I talk about the need both to do your homework and to trust your gut. Do these approaches seem contradictory to you? How can they work together? How might doing your homework—putting in the time to research and learn what you need to—help you confirm what your gut is telling you?

3. How does Peter's story—which includes both big failures and big successes—encourage you as you look at your own less-than-perfect life? How can Jesus' response to Peter reassure us when we are hung up on our own failures?

4. How do you typically react to failure—as something to fear and avoid or as something that's a necessary part of life? What might it look like for you to own your mistakes and see them as learning opportunities? As you look toward new challenges ahead, write down a few ideas for how reframing your view of failure can help you grow.

Chapter 6

FIGHT IN YOUR OWN ARMOR

MAKING THE MOST OF THE GIFTS
GOD HAS GIVEN YOU

Back in the early days of KMM, when I was struggling to keep my head above water, I briefly explored the idea of joining an established agency. I spoke with several of them. They'd brag about their client list and talk about benefits, expense accounts, and support staff. To be honest, it sounded wonderful—definitely better and *easier* than trying to go it alone. Then we'd get to the part of the discussion where they would start talking about their business model, and all of a sudden, working for one of the big agencies didn't sound nearly as appetizing. I heard about questionable business practices, shady associates, a strict focus on signing only marquee clients, and a culture that just didn't mesh with my values.

Many of these agencies talked about doing "whatever it takes" to entice clients to sign with them, but they didn't seem to genuinely care about those clients . . . or about fulfilling the grandiose promises made during the recruiting process. After landing prized clients (who could then help them land more prized clients), they treated them as business units, not people. And the agencies seemed to care more about capitalizing on their clients' earning potential during their brief window of opportunity than they did about investing in them and taking care of their physical and emotional well-being over the long haul. Their approach seemed purely transactional. While the thought of having someone else cover my expenses, pay me a regular salary, and give me an automatic "in" with the higher-profile draft prospects was incredibly appealing, the lack of integrity that came across in those conversations did not sit well with me. I also became fully convinced I could provide the same (or better) representation, opportunities, and resources to my clients through my own company without sacrificing integrity and personal service.

At one point I reached out to a good friend of mine, Kevin Plank, for a little much-needed advice and encouragement. Kevin was a fellow entrepreneur who had started his own T-shirt company in his garage with some money he'd saved up in college. Even though the odds had been stacked against him, he'd had all the confidence in the world that his little company could compete with the likes of Nike, Adidas, and Reebok—and thrive. By the time Kevin and I met, his company, Under Armour, had grown into one of the most successful sports apparel manufacturers in the world.

Kevin knew *exactly* what it was like to be a little start-up competing in a land of giants, so I valued his opinion. More than that, I had known Kevin for years. *Surely*, I reasoned, *if anyone can appreciate what I'm going through and help me see a way forward, it's him.*

As we talked on the phone, I remember sitting on my back porch, explaining the challenges I'd been facing getting KMM off the ground. When I finished, I sat back, fully expecting him to say, "Okay, Kelli, here's what you need to do . . ." and then lay out a plan of attack. Instead, I got, "Kelli, why don't you stop trying to do this the hard way and just go work for one of the big boys?"

I was floored. How could Kevin, of all people, tell me to give up?

"I . . . what?" I stammered. "Are you serious? Kevin, is that the advice you would have given your twenty-four-year-old self when things got a little tough—give up and go work for Nike?"

The line was silent for a moment.

"You're right," he finally admitted. "I just hate to see you struggle so much. You're very talented, Kelli. You deserve better." Then he added, "If starting your own agency is what you really want to do, then keep at it. You'll get there."

Kevin wasn't telling me to give up on my calling. Far from it. He was just trying to offer me an easier way of going about it. But I wasn't interested in doing it the easy way. I wanted to do it the right way. I wanted to do it my way.

I couldn't bring myself to compromise my standards, my integrity, or my clients' well-being. That wasn't why I got into agenting. I got into it to shepherd and to mentor, not to wheel and deal. I did not want to move to New York or LA, where many major agencies are headquartered. I'm based in Oklahoma because that's my home. It's where my family is, and it's where I developed my passion for football. It's who I am. And between Oklahoma, Texas, and surrounding states within driving distance, I've got one of the best recruiting fields in the country right in my own backyard. And yes, I do tend to favor the underdog because I know what it's like to be one.

When most people think of a prototypical sports agent, they likely picture a big, loud, larger-than-life, show-me-the-money guy. Obviously, that's not me. In fact, people who meet me are often surprised that I'm a sports agent, and it's not just because I'm a woman. They'll say things like "You seem too nice. Don't you have to be tough to do that job?" or "How do you even convince players to sign with you?" I always smile because, frankly, I love being underestimated. No, I don't look like other agents. I don't act like other agents. And I don't talk like other agents. But I also happen to think that's what makes me a better agent. The perception is that bigger is better, but a lot of that is an illusion. There is nothing a big agency can provide my clients that I can't. In fact, with me, they get even more.

GENTLE GIANT

Back in 2010, I was representing a young defensive tackle named Gerald from the University of Oklahoma. Gerald was the first player I'd signed who was invited to participate in the Combine, and it ended up being quite the experience for both of us.

For starters, even though Gerald had traveled with the OU team dozens of times, he had never flown by himself before—or taken care of his own ticket, rental car, and hotel. So just after signing him, I flew with him to Phoenix, where he was set up to do his Combine preparation. Over the next few weeks, I flew back and forth from Oklahoma to Arizona to check on him and make sure his training was on schedule. As I left to fly to Indianapolis for the Combine, I assured him he could handle the trip to Indy just fine on his own, and that I would be there to meet him.

Unfortunately, Gerald's trip got off to a rocky start. When he got out of the taxi at the Phoenix airport, Gerald set his phone on the car roof while he collected his bags, and then the driver took off, Android and all. Around the time his flight was set to land, I got a call from an unfamiliar number—but I recognized the voice on the line.

"Hey, Kells, I don't have my phone. I just borrowed this phone to call you."

"Why don't you have your phone?" I asked, trying not to sound like I was panicking.

"I just don't have it." (He told me the full story later, after he got over his embarrassment.)

I assured him I would meet him at the player hotel in an hour with a new phone. This was arguably the most important week of his life, and he could not be without a phone. Teams would be trying to reach him, and so would I. I set out on foot in downtown Indianapolis, found an AT&T store, and set up Gerald's number on a new phone. As I handed it to him in the hotel lobby, he shot me a look that said, "A flip phone? You've gotta be kidding me."

I smirked and said, "This will remind you to never put your nice phone on top of a car again. Got it?"

He chuckled. "Thanks, Kells."

The next day, I had a few hours to kill while Gerald was going through his medical evaluations, so I decided to go shopping—this time, for myself. No sooner had I walked into Nordstrom than my phone rang. It was Gerald. On his brand-new flip phone. Crying.

"Kelli," he choked, "I don't know what to do. They want me to do an MRI. I can't do it, Kelli; I can't!"

"Gerald, calm down," I said slowly, exiting the store. "Why can't you do the MRI?"

"I just can't!" he said, crying. "I can't!" He was starting to hyperventilate.

That's when it hit me. "Gerald, are you claustrophobic?"

"Yes," he sobbed.

Frankly, I couldn't blame him for his reaction. MRI machines can be terrifying—like coffins. Loud coffins. For most MRIs, the patient has to stay inside a dark, enclosed tube, perfectly still, for up to ninety minutes, all while the machine bangs so loudly that most techs offer earplugs. Even if you're not claustrophobic, the machines can be frightening. On the other hand . . .

"Gerald, I'm afraid you're going to have to," I explained as calmly as possible. "If you don't, they might think you're trying to hide something, and that could really hurt you in the draft."

I listened for a response, but all I could hear was crying. There was only one thing to do.

"Gerald," I said, stepping to the curb to hail a cab, "where are you? Are you at the stadium?" I glanced at my watch. If there wasn't any traffic, I could be back at the stadium in five minutes.

"No," he choked. "I'm too big to fit in the ones they have here. They want me to go to the hospital. They're bringing a car around to take me there now. Please, Kells," he begged. "Can you come? Please?"

"Don't be ridiculous," I said, ducking into the back of the cab. "Of course I'll come. I'm on my way right now."

He took a labored breath. "Thank you, Kells."

"Don't worry, Gerald," I assured him. "I'll meet you at the hospital. You just relax, okay? Everything is going to be just fine."

Fifteen minutes later, I arrived at the hospital and rushed over to the MRI area, where I found Gerald in an exam gown, hands up against the wall, crying and muttering, "I can't do this . . . I can't do this," over and over again.

There was something surreal about seeing a hulking six-foot four-inch, three-hundred-pound defensive tackle trembling and sobbing uncontrollably. *Poor guy.* My heart just broke for him. He was terrified. He needed someone to give him a hug. He needed someone to tell him everything was going to be okay. He needed a mom.

Think back to when you were little. When you were hurt or scared or some other kid was picking on you, who did you turn to? Who defended you? Who took care of you? Mom.

Ironically, back when I first met with Gerald and his father (his mother had passed away just before Gerald's red-shirt freshman year at OU), his dad likened me to Deborah, the Old Testament prophet. She is the only female judge mentioned in the Bible, and she inspired the Israelites to victory over the Canaanites. (See Judges 4.)

"God can anoint women to do great things," he'd said to me.

So at that moment, I did what came naturally. I walked over to Gerald and tapped him on the shoulder. When he turned around, I pulled him into a giant bear hug and said, "Gerald, I promise you, no one in the history of MRI scans has ever been crushed in one of these machines. I know it's scary. I know it's tight. And I know it's loud. But you can do this. I know you can. I'm going to be right here with you the entire time."

"You promise?" he said, sniffing.

"I promise."

After a few more minutes of gentle reassurance both from me and the MRI tech, Gerald lay down in the machine. But every time the tech started up the scanner and it began its banging, Gerald would panic and start hitting the sides of the machine with his fists, screaming to get out.

The tech suggested that we give Gerald a sedative, but we didn't want anything in his system that might cause a false positive on his upcoming drug tests.

We tried everything. We played music and did visualization exercises. I tried to distract him by talking him through the draft and telling him how exciting it was going to be to play in a real NFL game, but nothing was working. Every time they slid him into the scanner and the banging began, Gerald just lost it.

Finally, after what felt like hours of constant struggling, I called it.

"Don't worry about it," I told Gerald. "We'll figure something out."

After Gerald got dressed, I took him back to the hotel, where he was scheduled to have dinner with some of the reps from the Detroit Lions. Poor guy was so physically and emotionally exhausted, he fell asleep in the cab.

While Gerald met with the Lions, I went back to my room and started calling all the area hospitals, trying to find one that had an open MRI machine. I finally found a place twenty minutes away, so after dinner, I picked Gerald up and said, "Okay, we're going to try this one more time."

Even though the machine was open on the sides, he was still struggling.

"I can't do it, Kelli," he pled. "I can't."

"Gerald, it's okay," I reassured him. "See? The sides are

open. You can see right out, and I'll be right over there." I pointed toward the window where I'd be able to observe from the next room.

He just shook his head. "No." Then he grabbed my hand, looked up at me, and said, "You need to stay in here with me."

I looked at the tech and mouthed, *Can I do that?*

The look on his face was priceless—a comical mix of disbelief and amusement. Don't get me wrong, I get it. Gerald and I were definitely an odd pairing—a huge, half-hysterical football player and a petite former beauty queen. Thank goodness, the tech agreed and brought over a chair.

I sat by Gerald's head for four hours, helping him lie still—*four hours* to get twenty minutes of motionless scanning time.

I told him jokes, sang to him, and did anything I could think of to distract him. I could see his lip quivering the entire time. I just sat there, rubbing the top of his head and reminding him that I was right there with him and that everything was going to be okay.

When we finished and Gerald went to get dressed, the tech, who had performed dozens of MRIs on professional athletes over the years, looked at me and said, "I have *never* seen an agent do that before."

A few minutes later I went out into the hall, where Gerald was talking to his dad on the flip phone.

"Dad," I overheard him say, "it felt like Mom was right there in the room with me."

So yes, the perception may be that bigger is better, or that you have to be a man to successfully manage male athletes, but I can assure you, there is not a male agent in this industry who would have rubbed his frightened client's forehead and sung to him for four hours to help him get through an MRI. And yet, I can't imagine *not* doing it. It's just the way I'm wired.

JUST BE YOU

Rarely if ever is there a one-size-fits-all approach to doing things. That's because God made every one of us unique. A great passage in Romans says:

> In his grace, God has given us different gifts for doing certain things well. . . . If your gift is serving others, serve them well. If you are a teacher, teach well. If your gift is to encourage others, be encouraging. If it is giving, give generously. If God has given you leadership ability, take the responsibility seriously. And if you have a gift for showing kindness to others, do it gladly.
>
> ROMANS 12:6-8

Rarely if ever is there a one-size-fits-all approach to doing things. That's because God made every one of us unique.

Things like encouragement, generosity, kindness, responsibility, loyalty, and integrity are intangible qualities that make you who you are, and they are part and parcel of what makes you uniquely qualified to do what you were created to do. Don't compromise those qualities; embrace them. Use them to your advantage.

God didn't wire me to spend the evening hobnobbing with NFL bigwigs at the bar in the Marriott while one of my clients was struggling to get through an emotional crisis. He wired me with compassion and gave me the maternal instincts to see Gerald through a difficult situation. If he hadn't gotten through that MRI, odds are, that would have ended his hopes of being a first-round pick in the NFL Draft—or maybe ever playing in the NFL at all. There is just too much money at stake in this industry for a team to roll the dice on a player they can't be certain is healthy enough to make it through the season. Gerald didn't need a flashy powerhouse agent telling him to "man up and deal with it." He needed someone with a different set of gifts and skills. If I had suppressed those instincts because "it's not what other agents would do," Gerald's life would have been negatively affected. Remember, God doesn't give us gifts just to benefit us but also to benefit others. When we don't use them, we aren't the only ones who suffer.

> *God doesn't give us gifts just to benefit us but also to benefit others. When we don't use them, we aren't the only ones who suffer.*

As if being a woman doesn't make me enough of an oddball in this business, I am also a Christian. My faith influences the way I interact with people, the way I conduct business, the way I handle conflict resolution, and the way I see the world. In the highly competitive, dog-eat-dog world of professional sports, some people—who are we kidding, a lot of people—consider that a weakness. But I see it as an asset. Think about it. If you were a young athlete just starting out, would you want an agent who might be willing to lie, cheat, or steal to get you a contract, or someone who will represent you honestly and with integrity?

For some clients, things like loyalty and integrity matter. For others, they don't. I may not win every client I go after, but then again, I may not be the right agent for every client. In many ways, signing with me requires my clients to go against the grain as well. But when the fit is right, everyone benefits.

As you're pursuing your calling, you may feel unqualified based on what you see others doing or what you *perceive* the qualifications of a certain vocation to be. But I promise you God does not call you to do something without giving you all of the gifts, skills, and resources you need to do it. Of course, you probably have more to learn, and you'll grow in your abilities, but at the core of who you are, you are a perfect fit for what God is asking you to do. Trust His wisdom and take the approach that feels right for *you*—even if it seems to go against the grain or runs counter to popular opinion.

A NOT-SO-GENTLE GIANT

Do you remember David, the shepherd we talked about back in chapter four who took on the giant Philistine warrior, Goliath? Well, I'd like to take a closer look at the moments leading up to that epic battle because there is a small yet pivotal element to the story that often gets overlooked.

In one corner we have Goliath, who Scripture tells us was more than nine feet tall (for reference, Shaquille O'Neal is seven foot one). "He wore a bronze helmet, and his bronze coat of mail weighed 125 pounds. He also wore bronze leg armor, and he carried a bronze javelin on his shoulder. The shaft of his spear was as heavy and thick as a weaver's beam, tipped with an iron spearhead that weighed 15 pounds." And as if that weren't enough, "His armor bearer walked ahead of him carrying a shield" (1 Samuel 17:5-7).

In the other corner, we have David, a wiry yet determined teenager "armed only with his shepherd's staff and sling" (verse 40).

Doesn't sound like much of a matchup. In fact, when David's oldest brother figured out that David planned to take on the Philistine, Scripture says he became angry. Perhaps he said something like, "You're only a teenager. You aren't trained to fight this warrior."

Not even King Saul thought David stood a chance. "Don't be ridiculous!" he said when David volunteered. "There's no way you can fight this Philistine and possibly win! You're only a boy, and he's been a man of war since his youth" (verse 33).

But David, who knew God had called him to greatness, insisted. Now, *this* is where the story gets really interesting. Before sending David off to battle Goliath, King Saul gave David his personal armor to wear—"a bronze helmet and a coat of mail" (verse 38). According to Scripture, David "put [the king's armor] on, strapped the sword over it, and took a step or two to see what it was like, for he had never worn such things before" (verse 39).

Then, in what must have looked to everyone around him like an act of sheer idiocy, David turned to King Saul and said, "I can't go in these. I'm not used to them" (verse 39). He took off the king's armor, went over to a nearby stream, fished five smooth stones out of the water, dropped them in his shepherd's bag, and headed out to fight the Philistine.

I can only imagine the look on Saul's face when David opted for a handful of rocks over the royal sword and armor. But David knew what he was doing. The king's armor didn't fit. It didn't feel right. It wasn't, to use his own words, "proved" (KJV). David didn't want to take on Goliath the warrior's way or the king's way. Instead, David put his trust in God and the skills God had given him. He called upon the experiences that had prepared him for that moment. He told Saul: "When a lion or a bear comes to steal a lamb from the flock, I go after it with a club and rescue the lamb from its mouth. If the animal turns on me, I catch it by the jaw and club it to death. . . . The LORD who rescued me from the claws of the lion and the bear will rescue me from this Philistine!" (verses 34-35, 37). David wasn't trained as a warrior, but he was experienced with his shepherd's tools, and he knew that God had made him ready. When his moment of truth came, he chose to do it his way. He chose to fight in his own armor.

"You come to me with sword, spear, and javelin," David

proclaimed to Goliath, "but I come to you in the name of the Lord" (verse 45).

Then, as Goliath moved in for the kill, David reached into his bag, took out one of the stones, hurled it at Goliath with his slingshot, and hit him square in the middle of the forehead, killing him instantly.

"So David triumphed over the Philistine," the story concludes, "with only a sling and a stone, for he had no sword" (verse 50).

David knew he was well-equipped and that his experiences had uniquely prepared him for his moment of destiny. His unwavering belief in God, plus in the gifts and abilities God had given him, gave him the boldness and confidence he needed to succeed.

And you can do the same!

FIGHT IN YOUR OWN ARMOR

You are one of a kind. You have talents, aptitudes, and abilities that have been custom designed by the Creator Himself to help you be the best *you* you can be. That's the beauty of finding and pursuing your calling. You get to see how all the tiny, seemingly insignificant experiences you've had and the skills you've acquired over the course of your life come together to make something absolutely amazing.

Sure, I could smother the urge to give one of my hurting clients a big bear hug and instead let him figure out his own travel arrangements, replace his own lost cell phone, and deal with his own emotional breakdown, but then I wouldn't be me. I don't want to be a carbon copy of other agents. That's their calling. I want to be the agent God made *me* to be.

As you move forward on your own journey, be mindful of all the amazing gifts and experiences that have made you who you are. Embrace them. Be fully and completely you. Choose an approach that fits your personality, skills, and mindset, and when challenges come your way, trust in your own abilities and the God who gave them to you, believe in yourself, and always . . . *always* fight in your own armor.

DEVELOPING YOUR GAME PLAN

1. What are some characteristics that make you *you*? These could be personality traits, values, areas of interest, or life experiences. How do these things affect your approach to life in general and to your calling more specifically?

2. Reflect on Romans 12:6-8. Why do you think God gave different gifts to different people? How are our families, jobs, or communities strengthened by these varied strengths and approaches?

3. In what areas are you tempted to fight in someone else's armor by doing something the way you feel you're "supposed" to rather than the way that feels right for you? Conversely, can you identify any times in your life when you realized that your unique approach to a given task

was particularly effective? How can an experience like that affirm who God has made you to be?

4. How do you think God has equipped you for what He is calling you to do? How can you "fight in your own armor" with some of the challenges you're facing right now? Take a moment to think about what aspects of your past experiences, personality, or talents might have prepared you for what's ahead.

Chapter 7

DON'T BE AFRAID

CHOOSING FAITH OVER FEAR

I almost didn't go—and what a mistake that would have been.

It was 2006, and a friend had invited me to the annual Fellowship of Christian Athletes (FCA) Oklahoma state banquet. But after a long day at the law office, I honestly didn't feel like sitting through an evening of speakers topped off with "banquet food." Still, I have always loved the mission of FCA—to help coaches and athletes grow in relationship with Christ and positively influence those around them—so, at the last minute, I decided to attend.

When I took my seat in the magnificent ballroom of the National Cowboy and Western Heritage Museum that evening, I had no idea I was about to have an encounter that would change my life dramatically. Seated at the next table was a young man, a senior at Southeast High School in Oklahoma City, with his parents. His name was Gerald McCoy (yep—MRI Gerald), and he was the recipient of one of the awards to be presented that night.

I had heard his name before. Everyone who followed football in Oklahoma had heard of this talented young defensive lineman who had already committed to the University of Oklahoma. At eighteen years of age, he was already the size of a full-grown man—a very large, athletically built grown man.

Go talk to him, I told myself. But I was frozen in my chair, overanalyzing the situation and quickly talking myself *out* of this opportunity. *You don't know enough. You won't know what to say. You have no experience. Wait until you're more credible.*

It was my first full year as a certified sports agent, and as confident as I was in my knowledge and ability, I was still painfully aware of my lack of experience. Even the smallest step I took to connect with a potential client felt like a gigantic leap of faith.

As the evening went on, the self-talk in my head grew louder. *Why bother? He's only in high school. It's pointless to start a conversation now. You're not well-known enough. He won't even remember you in four years.*

Fear. I'd had so many battles with it in my life so far that I considered it my old nemesis. (More on that in chapter 8.) Like always, it was holding me back, keeping me in my seat. Keeping me from doing something I was entirely capable of doing.

"What is the opposite of fear?" a mentor once asked me.

"Courage," I responded confidently.

"No," he said. "I want you to look at this differently."

"How?" I asked. "If courage isn't the opposite of fear, what is?"

"Well," he said, "what if the opposite of fear is action?"

At first the statement didn't make any sense to me. If action was the opposite of anything, it was inaction. And what did inaction have to do with fear? But as I thought back over all the moments in my life when fear gripped me, I realized my mentor was one-hundred-percent correct.

Whenever I was afraid, I froze. The fear of making a mistake, saying or doing the wrong thing, or

> *Every time I overcame fear in my life, it was as a result of taking action.*

simply looking stupid rendered me incapable of doing anything at all. Conversely, I realized that every time I overcame fear in my life, it was as a result of taking action—dropping my agent application in the mail slot, sitting down to take that exam in a room full of men, standing up to that well-known agent who questioned my right to be at the Combine. In each instance, and in dozens of others, I faced fear head-on, and by taking action, I gained courage. My mentor was right. Taking action *was* the secret to overcoming fear.

During a break in the program that evening, I finally took action. Getting up from my seat, I forced myself to walk those few steps over to where the McCoys were seated.

Gerald had excused himself for the moment, so I introduced myself to his mother, Pat, first.

"Congratulations," I said, beaming and reaching out to shake her hand. "What a wonderful honor this is for your son—and for you!" I then introduced myself to his father, Gerald Sr.

"Such a pleasure to meet *you*, Miss Masters," he said, smiling warmly. As I would come to discover over the years, Mr. McCoy is one of the most thoughtful, friendly, engaging men on the planet.

When I handed Mr. McCoy one of my newly printed business cards, he held it in both hands as though it were a precious gift and studied the information on it.

"Wow!" he exclaimed. "Okay! I'm gonna keep this. I don't know what the Lord has in store, but you never know!"

We spoke a bit longer and I learned that we lived only five miles from each other. It was obvious that Gerald Sr. and Pat loved each other deeply and that they were incredibly proud of *all* their children. I liked them both instantly. I only met Gerald in passing that night, but his parents had made an indelible impression. When I said good night to them at the end of the evening, I knew I would see them again.

The following football season, Gerald redshirted at OU, which means he was able to practice with the team but didn't actually play in the games, giving him an extra year to grow and develop as a player and leaving him four more full years of football eligibility. Even though he was on the bench, his parents were at every single Oklahoma Sooners football game, both home and away, supporting their son and his teammates. After each game, I would pass by the area where players' parents waited to see their children, and I would simply say hello or give them a wave and a smile. And every time, they would graciously return the sentiment.

In late summer of that next year, Pat suddenly passed away. It was just at the beginning of two-a-day practices, and Gerald Jr. was beside himself, devastated. Sadly, because the NFLPA had passed a new regulation known as the "Junior Rule," prohibiting agents from making contact with a player or any person of influence in his life until he was more than three full football seasons past high school (a rule that has since been rescinded), I was unable to reach out directly to Gerald or his father. I did see his father at one game that season, from a distance. I gave him a look of condolence, put my hands over my heart, and mouthed, "I'm so sorry." I could only hope he understood. That was the last interaction I had with the McCoy family . . . until one fateful day years later.

I was attending a conference when my phone rang. It was Mr. McCoy. You could have knocked me over with a feather. I had honestly given up hope that I would ever hear from him again—especially now. Since I had last spoken to the McCoys, Gerald had become a superstar at OU, a consensus All-American, and was now a projected first-round pick in the draft. I had heard that every big agency was going after him and going after him hard. *Why would he want to talk to me?* I wondered. And yet, there Mr. McCoy was, calling to let me know he had kept my business card in his wallet all those years, and he was ready to meet.

"I want you to get the first meeting we take," he said.

A few weeks later, I found myself sitting across from Mr. McCoy, getting ready to launch into a full-blown presentation on why I would be an excellent fit as Gerald Jr.'s agent. But before I could even get started, Mr. McCoy stopped me.

"I want you to know something," he said. He looked straight into my eyes with such intensity it almost made me uncomfortable. "It does not matter to me that you're a woman. I want to hear what you have to say. You're just like Deborah in the Bible. And I want you to know that the fact that you're a woman is not going to affect our decision in any way. Do you understand that?"

Relieved that I didn't have to dedicate any time to defending my ability to be an agent and a woman at the same time (and yes, I do have a spiel for that), I launched into my game plan for Gerald Jr.'s career. The meeting lasted nearly four hours. And though I was exhausted by the end, I knew I had left it all on the field and had given myself the best chance possible to stay in the game.

That fall, I attended every OU home football game and virtually every away game. I made a point to see Mr. McCoy and Gerald after each game, talking to Mr. McCoy and reiterating important messages about the draft process, while simply giving Gerald a congratulatory hug or high five. Occasionally I'd get a kiss on the cheek along with his sisters. I felt like I'd become part of the McCoy family.

That spring, Gerald did, in fact, sign with me as one of his agents. Over the next several months, we changed each other's lives and literally made history.

The sights and sounds of Draft Day 2010 are so vivid in my memory that when I close my eyes I can still see and hear everything—the noise of the crowd both inside and outside Radio City Music Hall, the bright lights, the famous faces milling about in the greenroom. While most players watch the draft from home on TV, some of the top-ranked ones are invited to attend in person so they can appear onstage with the commissioner once they are selected. The venue is packed with fans, and the environment is electric. I was nervous, but I also had a great sense of peace. It was almost a certainty that Gerald would be chosen third overall by the Tampa Bay Buccaneers that evening, but we would have to wait for the call to be sure.

The room was filled with round tables covered with blue tablecloths and adorned with centerpieces featuring each invited player's name. Players, family members, and agents filled the chairs around the tables, ten per table, though many were too tense to stay seated for long. People chatted nervously. Several large television monitors were placed at the edges of the room so that we, along with the rest of America, could see the live broadcasts. As others started to file into the greenroom, I noted where the cameras were placed for ESPN and NFL Network and purposely sat far enough away to be out of the shot. And then . . . we waited.

When NFL Commissioner Roger Goodell walked to

the podium and the crowd began their traditional chorus of boos, my heart leaped. I had watched this moment on television year after year. Now, I was finally here. In person. With my client. The magnitude of this personal victory was overwhelming. The fact that I was "breaking a glass ceiling" as a female agent never even occurred to me. I was just trying to fulfill my calling and carry out my assignment.

The first pick, Sam Bradford, received his official phone call from the St. Louis Rams, and we watched as his table exploded with cheers and excitement. The second pick was named, and the tension in the room was palpable. After what seemed like hours, the call finally came from the Buccaneers. Gerald answered the phone and immediately covered his eyes with his hand. The rest of us at the table—his dad, his sisters, his daughter, his niece, and me—all began to cry too. He hung up the phone, still emotional, but with his big trademark grin spreading across his face. Seconds later, we heard, "With the third pick of the NFL Draft, the Tampa Bay Buccaneers select . . . Gerald McCoy, defensive tackle, Oklahoma." It was official! The hugs began and the tears started flowing again. I stepped back out of the way, letting Gerald soak in the experience with his tight-knit family.

Then, in true Gerald McCoy fashion, he walked onto that storied stage, arms spread wide, and picked up Goodell in a giant bear hug. The crowd loved it. And it started a tradition for newly drafted players that continues to this day. Unfortunately, I missed the whole thing because I was getting his family lined up offstage to go on for the official picture. But it didn't matter. It wasn't my night; it was his.

Later that night, I took the entire McCoy family out for steak and lobster to celebrate. When I finally checked my phone, there were well over a hundred calls and texts from friends across the industry. They had watched me persevere for years to see this day, and now they were rejoicing with me. It had been a long, hard-fought battle, filled with frustrations and disappointments, but I had finally made it. When Gerald was picked number three overall by the Buccaneers, I became the first female agent in NFL history to represent a top-five draft pick.

What if I had let fear win that evening years before at the FCA banquet? What if I had stayed glued to my chair and not introduced myself to Gerald's mother (something I later learned was important to both Gerald and his father)? Perhaps I would have still found a way to get a meeting with the McCoys the summer before his senior year. But, honestly, without the personal connection we'd established, it would have been highly unlikely. At that point, I hadn't signed a top draft pick and was still fighting to make a name for myself— and to be taken seriously. And my awareness of that almost ruined everything. I almost lost the opportunity of a lifetime because of negative self-talk, doubt, and fear. And goodness knows what would have happened to Gerald had we not been together during his fateful MRI a few months before the draft. In some ways, my fear almost cost him the opportunity of a lifetime as well.

ONE PERCENT BETTER

When I first became an agent, I was assured (mostly by people outside the industry), "You just need to get that first big client, and then the rest will come!"

I wish that were true. Every single year of recruiting is a fight. It takes intense effort, strategy, and almost perfect execution—that, and a ton of prayer. And each year there is an epic wrestling match inside of me between fear and faith.

I've been a football fan my whole life. And yet, when I first got involved in agenting, whenever I would turn on ESPN and listen to sportscasters analyze a game—not just the basics, but *really* analyze what was happening on the field, using all the professional insider jargon—I didn't get it. It was almost as though the analysts were speaking a different language. I was terrified of having to go into a meeting, a presentation, or even a casual dinner and talk football with someone who knew more about it than I did. Being a woman already put me at a disadvantage. Not being able to hold my own in a football conversation would just make it worse.

If anything, I felt as though I had to be *over*prepared. I've talked about grilling my friend Chris, the football coach, and getting information from scouts. I also went to Barnes & Noble and bought *Football for Dummies* (a great read, by the way). I spent hours watching old games, slowing them down and rewatching individual plays over and over again until I could see what the play-by-play guys were describing.

And then, after weeks of stressing myself into hysteria, I was sitting in a meeting with a high-level front office guy from the Dallas Cowboys, negotiating a contract for one of my clients, and a question came up regarding a clause in the current collective bargaining agreement. Being an attorney who lives for contracts and legal speak, I was fully aware of the clause and what it meant for my client—and the high-level executive wasn't. I was floored. I actually knew something that a front office guy with decades of experience in the league didn't. That's when I came to the realization that my fear was way out of proportion and holding me back. I was afraid of making a mistake, but actually I didn't have to know *everything* about football—at least not at the same level as a coach or offensive or defensive coordinator. I just needed to be an expert in the things *I* needed to be an expert on.

The same is true for everyone. Nobody starts off in a new job or career knowing everything. Most of my guys walk out of their first training camp with glazed expressions on their faces, muttering things like *It's all so fast. Everyone knows what they're doing except me. What if I'm not good enough?* Blake Jarwin was a phenomenal tight end in college, but he still had to learn the Cowboys' offense and get used to working with a new set of coaches, coordinators, and players. Many of us respond to new challenges with fear, and it takes time to gain confidence. That's why I always try to pair up my rookie clients with a veteran player—so they can be reminded that every player, even the Tom Bradys, J. J. Watts, and Khalil Macks of the world, was a rookie once too.

Be patient. Give yourself a break. Remember, not knowing what you're doing is part of the process. Don't let the fear of making a mistake or looking stupid stop you in your tracks. Don't self-talk yourself out of trying. Take action. Don't worry about getting it 100 percent right instantly. Just ask yourself, *What can I do one percent better today than I did yesterday?* When we try to fix everything at once, we get overwhelmed and wonder if we can succeed. But we can overcome those fears by taking action, one small change at a time. What's one improvement you can make? What little piece of advice can you implement today? You'll get there—as long as you don't let fear win.

One of my clients was the starting running back for the Ravens his second season, and he had a fantastic year. But the next season, something changed. Game after game, week after week, he was getting fewer and fewer touches. As the team's offensive scheme changed, he was simply being utilized less and less. He was frustrated, but because he was still relatively new, he was afraid to say anything. And that fear was slowly but surely stealing his career while he moped quietly on the sideline.

After one of his games I pulled him aside and said, "Listen, I know you're frustrated. I can see it from the stands. Have you tried talking to your coach?"

"I don't want to sound like I'm complaining," he said, shrugging.

"But if you don't say anything," I pressed, "how are they supposed to know what you're thinking? For all you know, they may be making assumptions about your attitude based on your body language or the look on your face."

He looked at me. "Yeah, but I don't want to be the guy who's whining all the time."

"Fair enough," I agreed. "But you need to be more proactive. Tell them that you respect the game plan, and you feel like you can contribute more. In other words, set it up as a 'What can I do?' as opposed to a 'Why aren't you giving me the opportunities?' Make it about the team. But if you don't say anything, that void will get filled up with the wrong stuff."

The next week in practice, he took action. He advocated for himself, and before he knew it, he was getting more opportunities.

The point is, if we're not careful, fear can render us helpless. We worry so much about saying or doing the wrong thing that we end up doing nothing. In many ways, that's even worse.

Fear, like pain, is part of the growth process. Every time you overcome one of your fears, you build strength, courage, and character. One of my favorite authors, Jon Acuff, once wrote: "Feeling afraid isn't failure. The arrival of fear is an invitation to be brave not a declaration of inadequacy."[1] We all need to be reminded of this as we face challenges in pursuit of our callings. And when the feelings of inadequacy come, we must learn to default not to fear but to faith.

STOP MAKING EXCUSES

When most people hear the name Moses, they likely picture a majestic Charlton Heston-like figure—sandals, woolen tunic, a long silvery mane billowing in the wind, and a massive stone tablet in each hand. Or they may picture him with his staff raised and a commanding expression on his face as he parts the Red Sea while the entire Egyptian army perishes at his feet. There's no question, Moses was one of the greatest, most formidable figures in the Old Testament. But he didn't start out that way.

Moses was born into slavery in Egypt. When Pharaoh decreed that all newborn boys of Hebrew descent be cast into the river and drowned, Moses' mother placed her baby boy in a basket and set him adrift along the banks of the Nile. He was rescued by Pharaoh's daughter, of all people, and was raised as an Egyptian prince. Then one day, years later, Moses saw an Egyptian beating a Hebrew slave, and he killed the Egyptian. Fearing he would be found out and punished, Moses fled Egypt, settled in the desert, married, and raised a family.

In the third chapter of Exodus, we read that Moses was tending his father-in-law's sheep near Mount Sinai when he happened upon a bush that was engulfed in flames yet was not burning up.

"'This is amazing,' Moses said to himself. 'Why isn't that bush burning up? I must go see it'" (verse 3).

When Moses approached the bush, he heard a voice coming from the flames. When he realized it was God, Moses was terrified, and he quickly covered his face in fear. Then God made a request. He said, "I have certainly seen the oppression of my people in Egypt. I have heard their cries of distress because of their harsh slave drivers. . . . So I have come down to rescue them. . . . Now go, for I am sending *you* to Pharaoh. You must lead my people Israel out of Egypt" (verses 7-8, 10, emphasis added).

Frightened and unsure of himself, Moses did what, frankly, most of us would do. He started making excuses. "Who am I to appear before Pharaoh?" he asked. "Who am I to lead the people of Israel out of Egypt?" (verse 11).

Even though Moses had been raised in the palace, Scripture is clear that he left Egypt under less-than-ideal circumstances. It's understandable that he'd be reluctant to return, let alone start making all kinds of audacious demands about freeing the slaves, especially since he'd spent the past forty years working as a shepherd out in the desert—hardly a high-profile job.

But God assured him, "I will be with you" (verse 12).

Still, Moses doubted himself.

He said, "If I go to the people of Israel and tell them, 'The God of your ancestors has sent me to you,' they will ask me, 'What is his name?' Then what should I tell them?" (verse 13). In other words, "I don't know what to say."

Once again, God countered, "Tell them, 'Yahweh, the God of your ancestors—the God of Abraham, Isaac, and Jacob—has appeared to me. He told me, "I have been watching closely, and I see how the Egyptians are treating you. I have promised to rescue you from your oppression in Egypt. I will lead you to a land flowing with milk and honey. . . ."' The elders of Israel will accept your message" (verses 16-18).

Even then—even with God Himself giving him the words to say and assuring him the people would believe him—Moses doubted himself: "What if they won't believe me or listen to me? What if they say, 'The LORD never appeared to you'?" (4:1). By the way, you may notice that Moses' insecurity had now dribbled over into a whole other chapter. And yet, once again, God refused to let Moses off the hook. In fact, He gave him two separate miracles to perform—the first, turning his staff into a snake, and the second, making his own hand wither with leprosy and then heal itself—as proof.

And *still* Moses doubted himself.

"O Lord, I'm not very good with words. I never have been, and I'm not now, even though you have spoken to me. I get tongue-tied, and my words get tangled," he said (verse 10).

At this point, it seems that God was starting to get a little hot under the collar—understandably so. He had already given Moses assurance, words to use, and miracles to perform, and now Moses was essentially saying, "I'm really not a very good public speaker."

"Who makes a person's mouth?" God retorted. "Who decides whether people speak or do not speak, hear or do not hear, see or do not see? Is it not I, the LORD? Now go! I will be with you as you speak, and I will instruct you in what to say" (verses 11-12).

Moses had to be out of excuses by now, right? God had given him every assurance and every tool he needed to successfully complete his task. But doubt and fear can be powerful demotivators, as is evidenced through Moses' final request:"Lord, please!" Moses pleaded. "Send anyone else" (verse 13).

It's difficult to reconcile the majestic image of Moses leading the Israelites out of Egypt with the fearful, self-doubting shepherd desperately pleading his case for a proxy with a fiery shrub. And yet God believed in Moses. He knew what Moses was capable of with His help, and He knew that when the time was right, Moses would rise up and become the leader the Israelites needed him to be.

Our belief in ourselves may waver, but God's belief in us never falters.

Our belief in ourselves may waver, but God's belief in us never falters. We just need to have the same faith in ourselves that God does. And the key to that is realizing that it's not about us. It's not about our weaknesses or what we can't do; it's about God's strength and what *He* can do. As Paul says in Philippians 4:13, "I can do all this through him who gives me strength" (NIV).

As time went on, Moses saw God working through him, giving him the words, the wisdom, and the courage to accomplish what by himself would have been impossible. And as his faith continued to grow, so, too, did his impact. Moses may have started out as a slave, set adrift, fleeing and fighting his fate, but once he leaned into his assignment and put his faith in God, his life and the lives of millions of others were completely transformed.

We don't have to be perfect; we just have to be willing. God will get us where we need to be. Our job is to have faith in Him.

HAVE A LITTLE FAITH

Faith. Such a little yet powerful word. Second Corinthians 5:6-7 says, "So we are always confident . . . for we walk by faith, not by sight" (NKJV). But what exactly is faith? And how do we learn to walk by faith—even when we are dealing with fear? Well, first we must realize that faith is a real thing, not some flowery idea, ethereal concept, or wishful thinking. The Bible describes it this way: "Now faith is the substance of things hoped for, the evidence of things not seen" (Hebrews 11:1, NKJV). Did you get that? It's a "substance." It is "evidence." That means it's tangible. And like a muscle, the more it gets used, the more it grows. Faith is the action that counteracts fear.

Fear, on the other hand, is a spirit . . . but not a good spirit—and definitely not from God. In fact, 2 Timothy 1:7 says, "For God has not given us a spirit of fear and timidity, but of power, love, and self-discipline." God only gives us things that are good for us. He doesn't want us to be afraid. He wants us to conquer fear. And how do we do that? With faith.

Faith *does* come from God. It is what God gives us as evidence that His promises will come to pass. Faith is the fuel for our belief in God's goodness. When fear tries to lock us up and knock us off the path God has set us on, God gives us faith in Him, which allows us to take action, overcome our fear, and live productively as we pursue our callings.

More good news: Just as faith is real, so, too, are there real things you can do to help you walk in faith on a daily basis.

First and foremost, pray. Begin your day by spending time with God. There are plenty of great devotionals out there to help you develop a solid prayer life, but for me, prayer is simply about setting aside some time every day to connect with God. Start by thanking Him for all of the good things in your life—your family, your friends, your health. Then tell Him what you need, and ask for wisdom to make the right decisions, strength to deal with whatever challenges you might be facing, courage to move ahead despite your fears, and forgiveness for areas where you've stumbled. Ask God to help you organize your day so that you can do everything that needs to be done. Then listen. God may speak quietly to our hearts through His still, small voice, or He may speak to us through Scripture. As we listen and get to know Him better, we understand more about where He might be leading us and what we should ask Him for. The Bible tells us, "You can pray for anything, and if you believe that you've received it, it will be yours" (Mark 11:24), and I believe that wholeheartedly. Whenever I take the time to meet with God first thing in the morning, I find that my day is infinitely more productive. I'm more focused and less fearful. I'm more present. And I'm more clearheaded and able to take action on what's most important.

Second, write. Whether it's journaling, making lists, or

just getting your thoughts down on paper, writing (with a pen or pencil—trust me; it's far more therapeutic than typing at a keyboard) is an important activity for your mental health and productivity. Like prayer, writing helps you organize your thoughts, see what's lying in front of you, and think through the best path forward. If you struggle with fear, try writing down what you're afraid of. Seeing it in black-and-white can help you gain some perspective and can give you the opportunity to brainstorm how to respond to your fears with greater faith. As you do this, you could even combine writing with prayer and write letters to God, asking Him to help you live with greater trust and self-confidence. It's always fun to go back through old journals and letters to see how far you've come from one year to the next. Remembering how God has helped us in the past builds our faith for the future.

Another aspect to a faith-filled, productive life is to eliminate wasteful activity. Instead of mindlessly listening to the radio, watching TV, or scrolling through social media—all of which can magnify our fears and self-doubts—read a book, listen to an uplifting podcast, or watch a DIY tutorial. Spend time with actual humans. Make connections. Find or be a mentor. You'll be amazed at how many opportunities are out there to learn and grow, improve yourself, and help others. Living with purpose can build our faith and help us remember what matters.

Exercise can also help. Do something active every day. It doesn't have to be excessive; I'm not saying you have to start training for a marathon or power lifting at Gold's Gym.

Just get your body moving. Take a walk. Go for a bike ride. Putter around in your garden. Not only is it great for your physical fitness; it also has immense emotional and mental benefits, helping you be more resilient, optimistic, and grateful. When we have enough emotional reserve, it's easier for us to respond to life with faith instead of fear.

Finally, it's important to remember that faith is not a *sometimes* thing; it's an all-the-time thing. It is not merely an antidote when things go bad. It isn't something you talk about only on Sundays. If you want to live a life of purpose that's free from fear, trust God. That's where your strength and power will come from. He's not asking us to walk perfectly but rather to seek Him with persistence. And the book of Hebrews promises that "he rewards those who earnestly seek him" (Hebrews 11:6, NIV). What could be better than that?

I'm not saying life automatically becomes perfect and easy simply because you choose to walk by faith. You will still encounter obstacles. You'll still stumble from time to time, and fear will still whisper in your ear in moments of indecision. But with faith, you have the power to overcome fear because you believe in a God who is stronger than fear. You have the power to live out your purpose because you trust in the God who gave you that purpose. You have the power to overcome anything the world throws at you because you trust in the power of the almighty God. You don't have to worry about whether you are smart enough or strong enough. With God, you are always enough. That is His promise. And God always keeps His promises.

DEVELOPING YOUR GAME PLAN

1. How do fears—of failure, of inadequacy, or of injury—affect your daily life? How could choosing to take action help you move forward in courage?

2. How do you think Moses was able to change into the dynamic leader who later led his people out of Egypt? How can his story encourage you as you face your own fears about living with purpose?

3. When we let our fears talk us out of pursuing our callings, other people can suffer. Can you think of an example from your life when you might have missed out on having a positive influence on someone else because you were afraid? How might it be easier to think about facing your fears for the sake of others rather than for your own sake?

4. What role does faith play in your life? How can you build your faith? Look again at my 4 suggestions on pages 143–145 and think about which ones you might be able to implement. What additional ideas do you have?

Chapter 8

YOU ARE MORE THAN WHAT YOU DO

KNOWING WHO YOU ARE

By March of 1997, I had reached the end of my rope. My life, which for all intents and purposes looked perfect from the outside, was in actuality in shambles. At twenty-three years old, I had racked up an impressive list of accomplishments. I was a straight-A student, valedictorian of my class, a world champion baton twirler, and a beauty contest winner. But despite everything I had achieved, I didn't feel any real sense of accomplishment. Somehow, it all just rang hollow. Not that anyone would have known that. I did my best to put up a happy front—always smiling, always upbeat, never a negative word or complaint. Meanwhile, internally, I was consumed with shame and dread.

My entire young life I lived in fear: fear of failing, fear of letting people down, fear of not being good enough. I was the consummate people-pleaser, driven by a fierce desire to be perfect. My entire self-worth was wrapped up in my ability to perform, to win over an audience, and to earn more first-place trophies, which in hindsight was kind of ridiculous. I mean, who really cared if I dropped a baton, got a B, or came in second?

I did. In my mind, if I didn't live up to the very highest expectations, both my own and those of others, the world would come to a fiery end, and life as I knew it would be over. As long as I did everything right—aced every test, won every competition, always looked perfect (hair, skin, nails, clothes, weight, etc.), everyone would be happy, and everyone would love me. Talk about a recipe for disaster. Not only was all the constant preening and pretending exhausting, but I lived in terror that the flawless facade I'd spent years perfecting would crumble at any minute, exposing me for the fraud I believed I was. But then something happened that changed the course of my life forever.

IT'S JUST WHAT YOU DO

When I was little, my parents were Methodists. I, of course, had no idea what that meant. All I knew was that we went to church together every Sunday. When I was nine, we moved and started attending a Baptist church—mostly because my dad really liked the music. Clearly, we weren't sticklers when it came to denominational distinctions. Like with the Methodist church, we still went every week as a family, and I was baptized there and eventually joined the choir. Although we were regular attendees, my family wasn't overly spiritual. Going to church is just what you did in the Bible belt—a component of your social life. To that end, I don't remember us ever really talking about God or Jesus outside of church. It was just something we did on Sundays.

That's not to say I didn't understand the Bible. I knew the gospel story from the manger all the way through to the Resurrection. But faith wasn't a day-by-day, hour-by-hour concern. I just went to church because my parents did.

Once, when I was in grade school, I went to a little front yard Bible study hosted by our neighbor, who was a pastor, and his wife. There were a handful of kids there that day, and at one point the pastor's wife asked us, "Who would like to have a relationship with God?"

Even though I didn't really understand what she meant, I raised my hand. Then she led us in a little prayer. It was exciting, but it certainly wasn't life changing.

As I got older, I wrestled more with the idea of God. *Was He real? Did all of those things in the Bible—the Garden of Eden, the Flood, the parting of the Red Sea, the miracles—really happen?*

And then there was Jesus. I had heard people talk about having a personal relationship with Him, but something about that just felt so unattainable to me—like I wasn't special enough. I tried to be a good person, to say and do all the right things, but there was always a wrestling in my mind:

Am I doing enough? Am I good enough? I was so performance minded, I thought I had to earn a relationship with God. I just didn't know how. It wasn't as though I was running in the opposite direction from Him. I just didn't know how to move toward Him.

By the time I graduated from college, I was engaged to be married. My fiancé was a baseball player who had been drafted by the Oakland A's. As it happened, he was also an atheist. Needless to say, my parents weren't thrilled. I tried to get him to come to church with me, but my own faith was still so weak, I wasn't able to make much headway. I was also working a ton of hours while attending law school full-time. My life felt frantic and stagnant at the same time.

One night, as I was driving home from an evening work function, I turned on the radio, which was tuned to a Christian station. As I listened to the music, the full reality of my situation hit me, and I started to cry. I couldn't get my fiancé to embrace my faith or my family to embrace my fiancé. I was running myself ragged at work, and every combative, cutthroat hearing or deposition I sat in on made me question more and more if law was even the right field for someone like me. I was miserable and felt as if I was failing at every turn. Spiritually speaking, it was the perfect storm.

The next morning, I went to church. I honestly couldn't tell you what the sermon was about that day, but at the end of the service, when the pastor called everyone who wanted to surrender their lives to the Lord to come forward for prayer, I rose from my seat and joined them. The prayer was lovely, but I was so emotionally muddled, the words just felt like words—all except one: *surrender*.

That sounds so good to me right now, I thought. I was so exhausted, the idea of surrendering everything to God felt, frankly, like an answer to prayer. So when I got back to my apartment that afternoon, I did just that. I dropped to my knees in the middle of the living room and poured out my heart to God.

God, I don't know what to do. I don't know if I'm supposed to be engaged. I don't even know if I'm supposed to be in law school. I'm just so tired of always trying to earn the approval of everyone around me. I'm tired of trying to be perfect all the time because no matter what I do, it's never going to be enough. I just want to know that You're real and that You love me and that I don't have to do anything to earn that.

After a lifetime of pretending and performing, I had finally come clean and admitted that I wasn't perfect, nor was I ever going to be. And when that decision was made—when I realized I did not have to please anyone else or hide my flaws and failures—it was as if I had been released from a secret prison.

In that moment, God became real to me. There was no blinding light, no booming voice, no dove descending from the clouds. All I know is that as I knelt there on my living room carpet, crying and asking for God's help, His love for me became palpable. It became real. And it not only changed my heart; it radically changed my perspective. I realized I didn't have to do anything to get God to love me or approve of me. I wasn't just the sum of my achievements. I was more—I was

God's child. From that point on, I sought God's wisdom on every decision. My heart's desire was simply to follow God wherever He led me and discover His plan for my life.

At first I thought I was called to be a missionary. After all, that's what people who are looking to fulfill a spiritual calling do, right? But after spending several weeks fasting and praying, I felt God calling me to finish law school. I had no idea where my legal career might lead or how it would intertwine with God's plan, but for the first time in my life, I knew I was headed in the right direction—and for all the right reasons.

AGENT OF CHANGE

When I made the decision to put my life in God's hands, I discovered I did in fact have a purpose for being on this earth, and that purpose was much bigger than simply being an attorney—or, for that matter, being an agent. Being a lawyer and an agent may be my job, but it's not who I am. Yes, I understand the legalities of the NFL's collective bargaining agreement (CBA), but anyone with a law degree and a week or two alone with a copy of the CBA could do that. What makes me *me* are the specific God-given passions and values I bring to the table:

- My faith
- A strong desire to serve others
- A passion for mentoring and positively impacting young lives
- A deep need for justice

YOU ARE MORE THAN WHAT YOU DO

- A deep-seated drive to advocate for the people and causes I care about
- And, of course, a love of sports—both as a participant and a fan because I see the impact players can have on others

When people ask me what I do for a living, the short answer is "I'm a sports agent." But the truth is I'm also an advocate, a mentor, an encourager, a teacher, a counselor, a confidant, a manager, a shoulder to cry on, a "mom away from home," and a friend. And that's just the tip of the iceberg. I'm also a wife, a stepmom, a sister, a daughter, a colleague, a business woman, an adjunct professor, an inspirational speaker, and, perhaps most important, a child of God.

Yes, I negotiate contracts and help my clients get ready for the draft, but I also lead mission trips, mentor young women, pour into my family, support and encourage my friends, volunteer in my community, and am active in my church. I'm diligent, determined, competitive, compassionate, loyal, tenacious, generous, loving, and honest to a fault. All of these things (and more) make up who I am, and while they certainly don't show up on a business card, they *do* impact how I do business, how I care for my clients, and how I interact with others in the industry.

That's the beauty of putting your life in God's hands. He finds a way to use all of it—everything

That's the beauty of putting your life in God's hands. He finds a way to use all of it.

you've experienced, everything that makes you *you*. You are never limited to just one thing because God isn't limited by *anything*. With God in the driver's seat, the possibilities are, quite literally, endless.

DEFINING MOMENT

Over the years, many of my clients have gone through a similar process of self-discovery. Every single player I work with is driven and talented; if he weren't, he would not be among the one percent of college players who have an opportunity to play in the NFL. Many of them also see the bigger picture: the impact they can make with their platforms, the good they can do off the field with their resources, and the need to plan for life beyond their relatively brief professional playing careers. However, at some point, they all have to discover their true identity, purpose, and calling *beyond the game.*

When potential NFL draft picks are evaluated by coaches, scouts, and general managers, they are almost always asked some variation of the same question: "Do you love football?" Of course, they have to answer yes and do so convincingly. When NFL teams are evaluating players to determine whether they want to draft them and, if so, in what round, they want to know that the player is all in, fully committed, 100 percent. They want to see a young man whose number-one goal is to play football at the highest level and who has no distractions or outside interests that could undermine this commitment. That means that players are pretty much required to center their entire lives around football. Who they are as players becomes who they think they are as people. Making matters worse, a monetary value is assigned to them based on their ability to play the game. Salaries and signing bonuses for drafted players are supposed to be confidential but usually end up becoming public, so it's easy for guys to see how the NFL believes they stack up against everyone else. Not only is their entire identity wrapped up in football but so is their sense of self-worth.

The problem is, sooner or later, every professional football career comes to an end. Whether it's because the player is injured or simply gets older, slows down, and becomes replaceable, there comes a time when every athlete realizes that the door is closing on his career. If that player does not have a sense of purpose or see the value in his life *off* the field, the end of his football career can feel like the end of the world. *If I'm not a quarterback/tight end/running back/offensive lineman for the Cowboys/Eagles/Broncos/Jets, then what am I?*

That's why, from the very first time we meet, I make sure every one of my clients knows that I value him as a person— that beyond his production on the field, postseason honors, draft grade, all-star game invites, and draft projections, he is a unique human being with a special purpose beyond football. From day one, we talk about who he is as a person, his likes and dislikes, what drives him, what inspires him, who he looks up to, his hopes, his dreams, and what he wants to accomplish in his life. These guys already know what they can do on the field. Most of them have memorized every stat they've accumulated since their Pop Warner days. I want them to form a complete picture of themselves—their passions, their values, their gifts and abilities—so they can start to create a stat sheet of everything they have to offer *off* the field.

I want them to understand that while football is an important part of their lives right now, most NFL careers are short-lived, and odds are, they will still be young men when they retire. I want them to understand that while playing in the NFL may be their current assignment, it is not who they are. It does not define them.

CHALLENGE ACCEPTED

One of my most unique clients to date has been Alex Collins, a running back with a penchant for—of all things—Irish dancing. His high school coach and the coach's wife had taken Alex in during his high school years, and their younger daughter, Bryanne, was a dedicated competitive Irish dancer.

While he was training for the NFL Combine, Alex often drove Bryanne to dance class and sometimes stayed to watch. "You couldn't make it through my warm-up routine!" she teased her "adopted" big brother one day when they arrived at class.

"Wanna bet?" he retorted. Challenge accepted.

Several minutes later, doubled over and sweating profusely, Alex gasped for air. "This is harder than I thought it would be!"

Bryanne and about a half dozen of her fellow dancers burst into laughter. "I told you!" she snickered. "And we're just getting started."

The 5'10" running back, who had bulging muscles and long dreadlocks tied together loosely at the back of his neck, outweighed his fellow dancers by at least a hundred pounds. And though he was in the best shape of his life and considered one of the most elite college running backs in history, he was struggling through his first dance class.

And yet, in true Alex fashion, he was not going to be outdone by his classmates, and he refused to quit until he mastered the steps . . . no matter how long it took. Over and over, he glided across the floor diagonally, arms held firmly by his sides, then pivoted and traveled across the front of the room, spinning and kicking his heels into the air in unison with Bryanne, who was dancing by his side. Later that afternoon, a cellphone video of the practice was posted to social media. It was shared by various media outlets throughout his draft process in 2016.

But it wasn't until 2017, when Alex took over as the starting running back for the Baltimore Ravens, that his Irish dancing video went viral. And when he finally scored his first touchdown, his highly anticipated end-zone celebration was—you guessed it—the dance he had learned alongside his precocious little sister. He became known across the league as "the Irish Dancer," and he embraced the moniker, continuing to work on his dancing skills. For Alex, it wasn't just a hobby or a dare from his sister. Dance training actually gave him a decided edge in his playmaking ability, enhancing his footwork and agility.

He already had a fan base from his college days as an

Arkansas Razorback, and he was rapidly earning a place in the hearts of Ravens fans as well. But his most enthusiastic, outspoken fans came from the tight-knit yet highly territorial world of Irish dance. Social media posts poured in from around the world, celebrating this NFL star who had embraced their passion as his own. In the middle of the outpouring came a request, posted on Twitter, from a mom in Iowa seeking encouragement for her son Carl. Apparently, Carl had been bullied unmercifully for his participation in Irish dance. He had become withdrawn, and his mother was deeply concerned. She simply tweeted:

Any advice for a 12yr old boy getting bullied for taking Irish dance lessons? Maybe a shoutout to dancer Carl from you would help?

Alex saw the tweet and responded:

Never stop doing the things you love because someone else doesn't agree. Chase your dreams Carl and don't let them stop you from being great!

Carl's mom was elated, and so was Carl. When she looked up the Ravens schedule, she realized the team would be playing a few weeks later in Minneapolis, within driving distance of their home in Des Moines. She went online to purchase tickets so her family could see Carl's new hero play in person. Without knowing she had bought tickets, I asked Alex if he wanted me to work on getting the young man and his family to a game so they could meet him. Alex loved the idea, and I went to work contacting the Ravens' public relations staff and, of course, Carl and his mother. Soon I was on the phone with a weeping mother who told me she couldn't believe what was happening.

"This has changed Carl's life," she gushed.

"How would you all like to meet Alex in person?" I asked.

"What? I just bought tickets to the Ravens game in Minnesota!" she cried.

"Perfect. I'll get everything set up," I told her confidently.

Sometimes it can be hard to pull off game-day experiences for fans. Players are focused on doing their jobs, not on get-ting tickets and passes for others. But reaching out to fans is part of the deal. In this case, Alex absolutely went above and beyond. He arranged for Carl's family to be on the sidelines before the game, and he even took the time to go over and give a pep talk to Carl and his little brother during warm-ups . . . something many players won't do. After the game, Alex invited the boys back down to the locker room area, where he presented each of them with game balls signed by the entire team, something he arranged entirely on his own.

Afterward I received thank-you after thank-you from Carl's mother.

"Alex literally saved my son. I have Carl back," she shared.

By showing kindness, Alex inspired not only Carl but countless other young people experiencing bullying in their own lives. Throughout that entire experience, Alex saw exactly what we had been talking about since the first moment I met him. His purpose in life extends so far beyond the game of football. Or Irish dancing. Both are clearly important, but they are only two of his assignments along the way. As long as he continues to pursue his calling with excellence, opportunities will continue to open up for him. Like his journey, he's just getting started.

FIGHTING CHANCE

Another athlete I have been blessed to represent is Justin Wren, a mixed martial arts fighter on the Bellator circuit. Before I met Justin, I can honestly say I never imagined representing an MMA fighter. In fact, it was hard for me to even watch the sport, which is sometimes known as cage fighting and involves combat between two players using techniques from boxing, wrestling, and various martial arts. But when I was introduced to Justin and heard his story, my heart melted, and I immediately knew I was supposed to represent him.

Justin's story is a long and winding path, but I have yet to meet an athlete with a clearer picture of his purpose and calling. Like Carl, Justin was bullied as a young boy. He tells his heartbreaking stories in detail in his own book, *Fight for the Forgotten*. As he grew older, he found an outlet for his anger and frustration by joining the school wrestling team, where he excelled. A few short years later, he found himself at the Olympic training center in Colorado, but an injury derailed his dreams of wrestling for the gold. And yet, he wasn't done fighting. After his injury healed, he turned his attention to a new sport, MMA, where he also excelled. But as he quickly rose through the ranks in the Ultimate Fighting Championship (UFC), his personal life began to spiral out of control. Drug addiction, depression, suicidal thoughts . . . he was consumed. Then an acquaintance convinced him to attend a men's conference that changed his life forever.

When Justin shares his testimony, he says, "God loved the mess out of me." He gave his life to Jesus and began a lifelong quest to know Him and love like Him. He says:

> I just prayed hard. . . . I said, "God, what do you want me to do? Do you want me to fight? Do you want me to do something else?" . . . And that's when I had the vision.
>
> I was dreaming even though I was awake, and I saw myself in . . . the jungle and there were these hurting people. They were sick and they were enslaved and they were thirsty and people just hated them. They were withering away with their ribs out. I saw them coughing up their lungs. It messed me up because I thought I was a crazy person.[1]

A few days later, he told his missionary friend Caleb about what he'd seen. "When I finally told him, he said, 'Oh yeah, that's the Pygmies.'"[2]

The Mbuti Pygmies are a tribe in the Congo that had been enslaved and almost forgotten. Justin spent the next five years traveling back and forth between the US and the Congo, living with the Pygmy people and fighting to restore their humanity. He was able to rescue many from slavery, and he worked with nonprofit organizations to bring lifesaving water wells and property ownership back to the Pygmies.

He returned to the cage to fight on the Bellator circuit in 2015 and is now focused on his work through the Justin Wren Foundation, with initiatives to combat bullying in the US and to restore the rights and dignity of slaves around the globe. He is not only fighting his opponents in the cage; he is fighting for something he truly believes in.

Both Alex and Justin understand that their jobs do not define who they are. Nor do their jobs determine their value. And if professional athletes are able to look beyond what they do in their high-profile, high-pressure jobs and discover their God-given calling in life, so can you.

IMPACT OF BIBLICAL PROPORTIONS

If you're looking for examples of people who were not defined by what they happened to do for a living, you don't have to look any further than the Bible. God is forever calling people to contributions well beyond their day jobs. In fact, some of the characters in the Bible with the greatest impact had some of the most common vocations.

We've already met David. He was a lowly shepherd working in his father's fields when he was tapped by God to become the future king of Israel. He not only defeated Goliath; he also later united the twelve tribes of Israel into one kingdom, established the capital city of Jerusalem, and is credited with writing many of the psalms. Not bad for a simple court musician and sheepherder. He didn't let his job limit him. Rather, he was faithful in his God-given assignments, and God propelled him to greatness, changing the course of history and positively impacting the lives of millions in the process.

God is forever calling people to contributions well beyond their day jobs.

Moses, of course, was also a humble shepherd, tending his father-in-law's flock when God called him to lead His people out of Egypt. Moses not only liberated the Israelites from slavery and led them on a forty-year journey to the Promised Land; he also authored the first five books of the Bible: Genesis, Exodus, Leviticus, Numbers, and Deuteronomy.

Ruth was a young widow from the land of Moab who worked in the fields to provide food for her mother-in-law, Naomi. But her faith and loyalty captured the attention of the landowner Boaz, and after they married, God honored her by making her the great-grandmother of King David.

Then there were the apostles. Andrew, Peter, James, and John were all fishermen when Jesus called them into ministry. Matthew was a tax collector, as was Zacchaeus, another follower of Jesus. Luke, not one of the original Twelve but still a disciple of Christ and author of one of the Gospels and the book of Acts, was a physician by trade. Yet despite their varied backgrounds, all of these men played a significant role as witnesses to Jesus' resurrection and as the first leaders of the early church.

Paul was a tentmaker. After encountering the newly resurrected Jesus on the road to Damascus, he traveled extensively across the Roman Empire spreading the gospel message, leading countless men and women to Christ. And of the twenty-seven books in the New Testament, Paul is credited with writing thirteen of them.

All of these individuals were born with a God-given purpose, yet up until the moment they were called, each was carrying out other, less glamorous assignments. Yet God used those assignments to mold and develop each of them into who they were meant to be. And when the time was right, each one stepped out in faith to follow Him, accomplishing far more than any of them likely dreamed possible.

Even age had no bearing on what these biblical figures achieved. Abraham was in his seventies when God called him to "leave your native country, your relatives, and your father's family," promising to "make [him] into a great nation" (Genesis 12:1-2). Moses was eighty when God spoke to him through the burning bush, and Noah was almost six hundred years old when God commissioned him to build the ark. On the other end of the spectrum, Esther and Mary were likely only teenagers when they were called for their respective tasks—Esther to become Queen of Persia and Mary to be the mother of Jesus.

And then, of course, there is Jesus Himself. Before he began His ministry, Jesus, like His father, Joseph, was a carpenter and, quite possibly, the most underestimated individual in all of human history. When Jesus came to teach at the synagogue in His hometown, many of the people in attendance, knowing of His profession, questioned the validity of His message. "What's this wisdom that has been given him?" they asked. "What are these remarkable miracles he is performing? Isn't this the carpenter?" (Mark 6:2-3, NIV). In their minds, someone who made furniture and buildings for a living simply wasn't capable of such wisdom and power. They had no idea He was really the Son of God. Talk about exceeding expectations!

In fact, Jesus' entire life was a lesson in subverting expectations. Even though the Jews had been waiting and watching for the Messiah for generations, nobody—save a small band of disciples—believed that Jesus, a simple carpenter from Nazareth, could possibly be the Savior they were waiting for. After all, He was born in relative obscurity to utterly unremarkable parents; He openly criticized the religious leaders of the day; He hung out with tax collectors, prostitutes, and lepers; He healed the sick on the Sabbath, in direct violation of the law of Moses; and, frankly, He didn't look the part. The prophet Isaiah is believed to have been prophesizing about Jesus when he said, "There was nothing beautiful or majestic about his appearance, nothing to attract us to him. He was despised and rejected—a man of sorrows, acquainted with deepest grief" (Isaiah 53:2-3). Definitely not the description of a king. And yet, almost two thousand years later, millions of people the world over still celebrate Jesus' birth; follow His teachings; share His message of love, hope, and forgiveness; claim Him as their personal Savior; and accept His promise of eternal life. Not a bad legacy for a carpenter.

RISE AND SHINE

Years ago, the US Navy ran an ad campaign around the tagline "It's not a job; it's an adventure." I can't think of a more fitting description of what it means to lean into your God-given assignments and follow your calling.

All of us are so much more than what we do for a living. No matter what vocation or avocation you pursue, there will always exist the opportunity to do more, to use your gifts in ways that benefit not just yourself but others as well.

Don't let yourself be limited by a job description or defined by someone else's expectations (or lack thereof). Lean into every assignment you are given, look for ways to expand your sphere of influence, and let God work through you.

Remember, pursuing your calling is a lifelong journey that doesn't end until you take your last breath. Whatever assignment you are currently engaged in is not a destination point. It's not the end of the road. It's just one in a series of God-ordained opportunities to make a difference, to leave a legacy, and to make your mark.

As Jesus said in His Sermon on the Mount, "You are the light of the world—like a city on a hilltop that cannot be hidden. No one lights a lamp and then puts it under a basket. Instead, a lamp is placed on a stand, where it gives light to everyone in the house. In the same way, let your good deeds shine out for all to see, so that everyone will praise your heavenly Father" (Matthew 5:14-16). You are called to be a light—to point others to God and get involved in His good work in the world. Let your light shine!

DEVELOPING YOUR GAME PLAN

1. Can you relate to my struggle to keep up a perfect facade and earn approval? How can it be freeing to admit our flaws to God? What do you think it means to surrender to God?

2. How do the stories of Moses, David, Ruth, the disciples, Mary, Esther, Paul, or my clients Alex and Justin remind you that you are more than your job? How do these stories inspire you as you seek your own bigger purpose?

3. When you look around you, where do you see God working in your community, church, or job? How could this intersect with your own passions and abilities? Where could you get involved in the meaningful things He's doing?

4. Take a minute to dream big. What kind of legacy would you like to leave? How would you like people to remember you? How can you let your light shine? Write down your thoughts and reread them when you need encouragement and inspiration.

Chapter 9
JUST TRUST GOD

FINDING HIS PURPOSE
FOR YOUR LIFE

The dream in my heart when I started my agency was not to make millions of dollars. In fact, becoming an agent had absolutely nothing to do with money. It was about impacting the lives of athletes—guiding and inspiring them to become great men, great leaders, and great members of society.

In 2013, I had the opportunity to watch that dream become a reality in a very tangible way—in the impoverished nation of Haiti.

I had arranged to take a group of my clients on a weeklong mission trip during the off-season. The athletes were a mix of rookie and veteran NFL players plus one of my Olympian clients, and some friends and other volunteers were coming along as well. I hoped that serving together in a different environment would give us all a chance to positively impact the people we met on the trip.

The night before we left, we all met up in Dallas for orientation and prayer. As the athletes filed into the meeting room of the airport hotel, I studied their faces and body language. Most of them were slumped down in their chairs, foreheads furrowed, scrolling through their phones. None of them looked joyful or excited. In fact, they were all visibly stressed—not about the trip but about life: responsibilities, pressure, bills to pay (with no off-season income), and challenging situations in their personal lives that were being exacerbated by their status as NFL players. All of them, to some extent, seemed to carry the weight of the world on their shoulders.

I must confess I was frustrated at first that they all seemed so distracted and disengaged. *Don't they realize what we are about to do?* I wondered. *Don't they realize how blessed they are compared to the people of Haiti, one of the most impoverished nations on the planet?*

But as I settled my soul and quietly prayed over every one of them before orientation began, God softened my heart. I realized that each of us had been brought together in that moment for a purpose far beyond my own plan for "impacting lives." Every one of us came from a different background, had different life experiences, and brought a unique mindset based on those backgrounds and experiences. God alone knew what each of us needed to learn on this trip and in what specific ways every one of us might contribute. He was working in my clients' hearts—and in mine, too. Who was I to judge them for struggling?

My change of heart was just the first shift in perspective on that trip. As the leadership team from Mission of Hope Haiti, the nonprofit organization coordinating the trip, educated us on the needs of the people we were about to go serve and instructed us on what we were going to do during our time away, I realized that this trip was not only exactly what my players needed; it was what I needed as well. We had all been dealing with so much stress that a healthy dose of perspective was way overdue.

Although I had traveled and served throughout my life, this would be my first visit to a third-world country. To be honest, as much as I admire and respect missionaries, up to this point in my life I had questioned the effectiveness of or need for short-term mission trips. After all, it was one thing to dedicate your life to serving in an impoverished community, but to just dip your toe in for a week and then leave? Somehow it seemed selfish or, at the very least, self-serving. But after much prayer and contemplation, I realized that a brief trip to Haiti was not meant to be a special accomplishment or the fulfillment of our call to serve but, rather, the beginning of something much greater and long-lasting. It was meant to challenge our view of the world and open our eyes permanently to the needs of others and the power we have, through obedience to God, to make an impact. I admonished my clients while also reminding myself, "Remember, this trip is not about you but about making a difference in the lives of others. And please don't call this a life-changing experience unless you actually plan *to change your life* as a result."

When we arrived in Haiti, I was struck by a sudden realization. When I surrendered my life to Christ, my initial desire was to do missions work. That led me to study non-profit law, which in turn led me to work with charitable foundations, which led to working with my first professional athlete, which led to becoming a certified agent, which led to starting my own agency. Now, here I was, doing mission work *through my own agency.* God had led me through a series of different assignments, all of which culminated in me being right where I had dreamed of being from the very beginning—only now, I was truly ready for it.

The sights and sounds of the capital city of Port-au-Prince overwhelmed us that first day. Everywhere we turned we saw human beings living in unimaginable circumstances. My concept of poverty was completely upended in a matter of hours. In America, most people who live in poverty still have a place to sleep at night and food to eat. The people we saw that day had literally nothing but the tattered clothes on their backs. Their "homes" were tiny shacks with dirt floors. Most people were malnourished, and some looked as though they hadn't eaten in days. As we passed through the crowded streets on a bus, I realized, *These are human beings, just like me. They have the same emotions. They have friends and families. They are capable of learning and dreaming and creating, just like any other human being born anywhere else on earth. And yet every last bit of their time and energy is spent fighting just to stay alive for another day.*

Eventually our group got settled at our "resort"—a cluster of simple bungalows situated outside of Port-au-Prince along a beautiful stretch of beach. We enjoyed a simple but filling dinner together and discussed our plans for the week ahead. But even as we laughed and smiled, none of us could get those first images out of our heads. Those initial few hours on the island had been sobering, to say the least.

The next morning, we all boarded the bus to go to church a few miles away. When we arrived at the open-air pavilion, it was already filled with Haitian people singing their praises to God. Virtually all of them had walked, some for miles, many on empty stomachs, to be in church that morning. As we made our way into the building for the service, dozens of smiling, singing, and laughing children ran to greet us. Once inside, I spotted a teenage girl sitting alone and immediately felt drawn to go sit beside her. She had a tiny baby on her lap, wrapped in a dingy towel. We smiled at each other as she raised the baby to her chest and stood to worship. I stood, too, and surveyed the attendees.

My athletes towered over the Haitians, and their athletic frames stood in stark contrast to the willow-thin natives. Their bewildered facial expressions made them even more distinguishable from the crowd. They watched as the people, whom we knew had nothing and lived in circumstances that seemed utterly hopeless, lifted their hands and voices to joyfully praise and give thanks to God. I could read the questions on my clients' faces, and they echoed my own: *How could these people possibly be so full of joy? So full of hope? So willing to trust and love God?*

The music from the tiny speaker at the front of the church grew louder as a slender young man stepped to the platform. He was wearing an ill-fitting suit—probably the only one he owned—but looked as if he had gone to great efforts to look his very best. His voice carried over the crowd as he joined in the final worship song of the morning:

I give myself away
So You can use me.[1]

Over and over, the crowd sang those words, written by William McDowell, an American gospel musician.

As I watched these beautiful people with no earthly possessions and no idea where their next meal was coming from sing to God about surrendering their lives, hearts, and hopes to Him, my heart melted. They knew what it meant to trust God *completely* in a way I never had. I watched the stress and frustrations of my athletes melt away, too, as we were all simultaneously convicted. We were so blessed. We had so much to be thankful for. Even the problems we experienced were mostly tied to the possessions we had in our lives. No wonder it was so easy for us not only to lose perspective but also to fail to rely fully on our faith in God.

Our morning at the Mission of Hope church in Haiti

affected us all. Our hearts were set for the week, and we spent the next several days pouring into orphans and adults throughout the area. We learned about the needs of the local communities and how to meet them. We delivered food and building supplies to villages and schools that did not have regular access to those provisions. We prepared and served meals, and we spent hours hugging and playing with orphaned children. We spent an entire day helping to collect and transport large stones from a riverbed to a plot of land where a school was to be built. We worked hard with smiles on our faces. And we each grew in our trust in God, our gratitude for His blessings, and our love for each other.

My players may have towered over the crowd that Sunday morning, but the light shining from within the people of Haiti as they cried out in song for God to use them to achieve His purpose was positively radiant. These people had virtually nothing, yet they were willing to give all they had to be part of God's plan. They weren't limited by their lack. Instead, they found freedom in God's provision.

That trip established an important precedent for my agency and our athletes: We would always put God's calling and purpose for our lives *first* and trust Him to lead us where He wants us to go. Trusting God is foundational for me and my agency. But more than that, it is the key to true fulfillment.

IT'S NOT *WHAT* YOU KNOW . . .

We are not all called to be in full-time ministry. But as I've said before, having a calling is not limited to ministry alone.

It's about discovering who you are meant to be, leaning into your passions, and using your unique blend of gifts and talents to make a difference in the lives of others. And all of that begins with knowing and trusting God.

That doesn't mean simply acknowledging that He exists. It means recognizing that He is our heavenly Father and accepting His love for us. That is where the journey toward purpose and identity starts. Once we accept Jesus as our Lord and Savior, the pursuit of our true calling can begin.

You've heard me talk about my own decision to follow Jesus. It was as simple as realizing that I was tired of trying to live the perfect life and acknowledging that I needed help. And while the image of me sobbing on my knees in my living room, admitting that I couldn't make it on my own, might look like a moment of weakness, it was actually a moment of great strength.

As I've mentioned, before surrendering my life to Jesus, I lived in constant fear—fear of failing, of letting people down, of having people discover that I didn't have it anywhere near as together as they thought, of being outed as a fraud. But from the moment I made the decision to stop trying to forge my own path and instead follow the course God had mapped out for me, that fear receded. I no longer live in fear of failing because I know that as long as I am following God's leading, failure is not possible. Sure, I'll make mistakes and mess up tasks. But by letting God be in charge of my life, I'll never fail at what is most important.

Pastor Tim Kizziar articulated this so well. He said, "Our

greatest fear . . . should not be of failure but of succeeding at things in life that don't really matter."[2]

I know a lot of people who are financially successful. They live in beautiful homes, drive expensive cars, eat in all the best restaurants, and wear only the finest clothing and jewelry. They are great at what they do, are at the top of their professions, and are admired by a lot of people. And do you know what? Many of them are absolutely miserable.

Money can buy a lot of things, but it can't buy fulfillment. You can't put a price tag on meaning. A truly meaningful and fulfilling life can only come when we are both connected and contributing to something bigger than ourselves.

That's where God comes in. God *is* the something bigger we need to connect to. Without God, every endeavor we undertake will come up short because our efforts will always be limited to what we alone can do. But "with God everything is possible" (Matthew 19:26). Think about it. He turned an insecure, tongue-tied shepherd into one of the greatest leaders in all of history. He gave a teenage girl the courage to save the Jewish nation. And He used a ragtag group of fishermen to launch a spiritual movement that has lasted more than two thousand years. Imagine what He has planned for you!

All you have to do is trust Him and follow Him. Pastor

> *A truly meaningful and fulfilling life can only come when we are both connected and contributing to something bigger than ourselves.*

and bestselling author Rick Warren once said, "Trusting God completely means having faith that he knows what is best for your life. You expect him to keep his promises, help you with problems, and do the impossible when necessary."[3] And He will. Just as He did with Moses, David, Esther, Joseph, and the apostles, the Bible assures us that "[God] is the faithful God who keeps his covenant for a thousand generations and lavishes his unfailing love on those who love him and obey his commands" (Deuteronomy 7:9).

If you are unsure of what to do, ask God. If you can't see a way forward, seek His wisdom. If one door closes, look to Him to lead you in another direction. One of my favorite passages in the Bible is Matthew 7:7-8: "Keep on asking, and you will receive what you ask for. Keep on seeking, and you will find. Keep on knocking, and the door will be opened to you. For everyone who asks, receives. Everyone who seeks, finds. And to everyone who knocks, the door will be opened." What a fantastic promise!

Even if we make a mistake, listen to the wrong people, or wander off the path, as long as we continue to ask, seek, and knock, and we stay attuned to God's voice, He can and *will* get us back on track. After all, it's not *our* mission He's trying to fulfill; it's His. Rick Warren phrases it beautifully:

It's not about you.
The purpose of your life is far greater than your own personal fulfillment, your peace of mind, or even your happiness. It's far greater than your

family, your career, or even your wildest dreams and ambitions. If you want to know why you were placed on this planet, you must begin with God. You were born *by* his purpose and *for* his purpose.[4]

"You were born *by* his purpose and *for* his purpose." That's why we can't do it alone. The truth is no genuine calling can exist apart from God. Everything we know, everything we are, and everything we are capable of is given to us by God for God. It's woven into our DNA, and it is activated the moment we surrender our lives to Him. The only way we can possibly fail is if we turn away from God and try to go it alone. Jesus said, "I am the vine; you are the branches. Those who remain in me, and I in them, will produce much fruit. For apart from me you can do nothing" (John 15:5).

> *The only way we can possibly fail is if we turn away from God and try to go it alone.*

So there you have it—everything or nothing. The choice is yours. But as someone who has spent time on both paths, I can assure you God's way is infinitely more rewarding.

YOUR MISSION, SHOULD YOU CHOOSE TO ACCEPT IT

If you're already traveling on God's path, I hope you'll take this chapter as encouragement to keep on going! Live in the freedom that comes from trusting your life and plans to God and being a part of His larger purpose. Find joy in fulfilling your calling as you follow Him.

If this is all new to you, though, you may be wondering, *So just how do I get onto God's path?* Honestly, it's as easy as asking. God created you. He wants to help you. Jesus Himself tells us, "You didn't choose me. I chose you" (John 15:16). The invitation has always been there. You just have to accept it.

And before you start making excuses, don't worry—God already knows you're not perfect. He already knows all of the mistakes you've made (and have yet to make) and all of your fears, weaknesses, and shortcomings—and none of it changes how He feels about you. The truth is we all fall short and need His forgiveness. That's why God sent His Son down to earth in the first place.

Jesus was fully God, yet He was born, He lived, and He died as a regular man so that He could share in every human experience. Just like us, He laughed, cried, ate, drank, slept, worked, hung out with His friends, got angry, was both loved and betrayed, and experienced great joy, great pain, and great sorrow. When He died on the cross, He took on all of our sins, shortcomings, and mistakes. Mark, one of Jesus' followers, put it this way: "The Son of Man came not to be served but to serve others and to give his life as a ransom for many" (Mark 10:45).

As an attorney, one of the best illustrations for this I can think of is that of a criminal appearing before a judge in a courtroom. The criminal has broken the law and therefore must be punished. For sake of argument, let's say the crime committed was murder. And since it's my backyard, let's say the murder was committed in Oklahoma, where they have the death penalty. By law, the judge has the right to sentence the criminal to death for his crime. But what if someone else agreed to take the full wrath of the judge and pay the ultimate price not only for this crime but for all crimes committed by everyone in the world—in perpetuity?

That's what Jesus did. By dying on the cross, He took on the full punishment we deserve so that we don't have to. Pretty amazing, right? It's even more amazing when you stop to consider that in His whole life, Jesus never actually sinned. He was completely innocent. And He still paid the ultimate price for us because He loves us—unconditionally.

The Bible says, "There is no greater love than to lay down one's life for one's friends" (John 15:13). Imagine loving someone so much you are willing to die on their behalf. That's what Jesus did. He paved the way for us—a completely fallen, sinful, and otherwise unworthy people—to have a relationship with our holy, perfect God. Jesus' death and resurrection cleared the path. If you want to walk on that path—if you're ready, like I was, to stop trying to go it alone—all you have to do is acknowledge Jesus' sacrifice.

The Bible clearly states, "If you openly declare that Jesus is Lord and believe in your heart that God raised him from the dead, you will be saved. For it is by believing in your heart that you are made right with God, and it is by openly declaring your faith that you are saved" (Romans 10:9-10).

There's no right or wrong way to make this commitment.

I made mine in tears on the living room floor in a moment of quiet desperation, and it certainly wasn't the most eloquent speech I'd ever made. But God's not looking for eloquence. He's looking for authenticity. Your words don't have to be perfect; they just have to be genuine.

Talk to Him. Tell Him what you're struggling with. Tell Him what you want. Ask for His forgiveness for what you've done wrong. Thank Him for everything He's given you up to this point—your friends, family, good health, gifts, and, of course, the extraordinary sacrifice He has already made on your behalf. Share the deepest desires of your heart. Welcome Him into your life. Ask Him to help you become more like Him and to give you opportunities to grow and to serve. Most important, don't let this be your only conversation with Him. He wants to be part of your daily life—let Him! Get to know Him better. Set aside some time every day to read about Him in the Bible. Invite Him into different parts of your day. Ask Him for advice. Thank Him when things go well and lean into Him when times get tough. Take the advice of David and "Commit everything you do to the Lord. Trust him, and he will help you" (Psalm 37:5).

And then . . . get ready for the adventure of a lifetime.

DEVELOPING YOUR GAME PLAN

1. Why do you think the Christians in Haiti were able to surrender themselves to God and trust Him when they

had so little? How can it be freeing to put ourselves in God's hands rather than striving to control our lives on our own?

2. In John 15:5, Jesus says, "Apart from me you can do nothing." Have you seen this play out in your own life? If so, how? What do you think it means to rely on Jesus?

3. If you haven't made a commitment to God, is that something you would consider? What might be holding you back? Think of someone you could talk to who might be able to encourage you. If you are following God's path, what difference has that made in your life? Are there more areas you need to surrender to Him?

4. What are some ways you can find fulfillment through being a part of God's bigger purpose? List a few things you think God might be calling you to do that can have a positive impact on the world.

Chapter 10

THANK YOU FOR BEING READY

STEPPING OUT IN FAITH

It's well known that Oklahoma's weather can be unpredictable; and in January, it can get downright dreary. That's why I'm thankful my job requires me to spend the first few weeks of the year somewhere warmer. In 2019, for instance, I flew down to Dallas to spend some time with three of my new clients. I had just signed Keaton Sutherland, a guard out of Texas A&M; Andrew Dowell, a linebacker out of Michigan State; and Jalen Guyton, a wide receiver from North Texas; and I'd arranged for all three to train together in Dallas leading up to the draft. Figuring they had probably been living on healthy prepared meals and occasional fast food, I invited them all out to dinner at one of my favorite steak houses. I also invited one of my veteran clients, Blake Jarwin. Blake had just finished his second season with the Cowboys, and I was hoping he would serve as a mentor to my new clients.

All four of them ordered the tomahawk steak, an enormous ribeye that still has about eight to ten inches of rib bone attached like an ax handle (hence the name). I had a salad.

After sharing a few war stories from their college days, the three new guys started drilling Blake with question after question about the draft, OTAs ("organized team activities," which are unofficial practices during the off-season), minicamp (a short training camp for new rookies held after the draft), his training regimen, and what it's like to play for the Cowboys. Blake was a good sport and did his best to answer everyone's questions between mouthfuls. It was just his second year in the league, so he knew how nervous, excited, and frightened they all were.

It's one thing for me to tell new clients what to expect through this process of transitioning to the NFL. It's another for them to hear it from someone who has just gone through it himself. As the evening continued, I was more than happy to sit back and let them talk.

We were in the middle of dessert when Jalen turned to me and said, "Miss Kelli, how long have you been an agent?"

"Well, let's see." I set my fork down. "I got certified back in 2005 . . ." *Wow,* I thought, *that seems like a lifetime ago. Most of these guys were probably only . . .* I caught myself. "Wait." I glanced around the table. "How old are you guys?"

A chorus of "Twenty-one" and "Twenty-two" emanated from the group. I quickly did the math in my head. *Twenty-two minus fourteen is . . . oh my gosh.*

Keaton leaned forward a bit in his chair, a concerned look on his face, and said, "Is something wrong?"

"No," I assured him. "Not at all. In fact, I just realized that you guys"—I gestured toward them—"are why I'm here." Confused glances abounded.

"You see," I began, "back in 2005, just before I sat down to take my certification exam, a vision popped into my head of a group of little boys playing football in their backyard. They couldn't have been more than seven or eight. It wasn't a formal league or anything. Just a group of neighborhood kids playing scratch football, pretending to be Peyton Manning, Reggie Wayne, or Brian Urlacher and dreaming about playing in the NFL someday. Those little boys were the reason I had spent months studying contracts and pouring over the collective bargaining agreement. Because someday, they were going to need me to help guide them through the draft, their first professional contract, and everything that comes after it. Those little boys needed me to be ready—ready to help them make that final roster; ready to help them make the most of their time in the NFL; ready to help them prepare for life *after* football; and ready to help them realize their dreams and become everything God intended them to be."

Breathless, I paused and took in each of their faces. "And I just now realized those little boys . . . were *you.*"

"That's so awesome," Blake said, beaming.

"Seriously, Kelli," Keaton agreed. "That's really cool."

It *was* cool. It *was* awesome. And as I sat at that table, surrounded by the grown-up little boys I'd envisioned fourteen years earlier, I knew, without a shadow of a doubt, that I had found my calling.

"Well . . ." Jalen smiled and raised his water glass. "On behalf of all of us, thank you—for being ready."

ARE YOU READY?

Remember the handsome former classmate of mine who was taking the agent exam at the same time I was? The one who already had future clients waiting in the wings? Well, it turns out he wasn't *quite* ready for the exam that day, and he failed. He took the exam again the next year and failed *again*.

Here's how it ended up playing out. He may have failed at becoming a sports agent, but he knew he was destined for something different . . . something even better suited to him. So he continued to learn and chase his passions. He eventually moved to California and built a company that would go on to produce award-winning movies. He refused to see failure as final, and now he has an enormous platform. His work reaches millions around the globe.

No matter what failures you've experienced, no matter what adversity you face, nothing—absolutely nothing—can keep you from your God-given destiny if you pursue it with all your heart. So how do you know you're on the right track, even when things get tough or life seems to be falling apart?

It starts with surrender. Stop letting fear dictate your

decisions. As I've talked about so much in this book and in my mentorship of others, fear keeps us from stepping out to fulfill our callings. It causes us to focus on what might go wrong rather than on what can be accomplished if we just have faith. Know that you have a divine

Nothing—absolutely nothing—can keep you from your God-given destiny if you pursue it with all your heart.

destiny and surrender yourself to it. For me, that meant giving my whole heart and life to God and trusting Him to guide me down the right path. Stop trying to control the things that are beyond your control, and embrace the power you have to fulfill your purpose.

Remember, only you can find your calling. You can't find it by looking at your circumstances, and no one else can dictate it to you. When you find it and pursue it, you will have peace on the inside, but chances are you'll still face adversity and opposition. What if I had given up on being an agent when I was told I would never be successful? Or when I ran out of money or had door after door (after door) slammed in my face? What if I had succumbed when I saw people posting vile things about me on the Internet, lying about me, or attacking my character? Yes, all of those things have happened. But they didn't deter me because I knew deep in my spirit that I was right where I was supposed to be, doing exactly what I was meant to do. I have fought too long and too hard to get to this place, and no one is going to take that peace away from me.

Accept the fact that adversity is going to be part of your story. You will experience failure and pain and setbacks. But if you are pursuing your purpose, those failures and setbacks will only make you stronger. You will learn what works and doesn't work. You will learn who to trust and who not to trust. You will learn to seek wise counsel and to embrace problems as opportunities. Nothing you go through—not even your own self-sabotage, missteps, and mistakes—will go to waste. When you trust God, everything is redeemable and every experience will move you one step closer to your calling.

Every part of you was designed by your Creator for a reason. You have experience, knowledge, and skills that make you different from every other person on the planet. As long as you are faithfully walking out your purpose and relying on God, you will be able to handle everything that comes your way because you were specifically wired to handle it. Even if it doesn't look like it right now, you have the connections and resources you need to succeed in whatever it is you have been called to accomplish. But you have to make the choice: You have to say yes to that calling and dedicate yourself to learning, to growing, and to pushing yourself outside of your comfort zone. You have to be willing to make all the sacrifices and take all the risks that will be required of you.

Just like David, and every other person I've highlighted from the Bible, you can be victorious by choosing to fight in your own armor. No matter what the world—or even your own negative thoughts—tells you, you do not need what anyone else has in order to be victorious. God has given you everything you need to succeed. Don't waste time and energy comparing your life to others. Everyone has their own unique calling. Focus on fulfilling yours and on helping others fulfill theirs.

Dedicate yourself to developing your talents and doing whatever it takes to achieve your goals. But remember that true fulfillment only comes when we dig deep. Know that we are more than what we do and that we each have an incredibly important role to play in God's plan for this world. Your worth is not limited to your current job, role, title, or tasks. It is part of a much bigger picture . . . and you are more powerful than you realize. If you keep this perspective, there is nothing and no one that can stop you.

You were born for such a time as this. Now, go do what you were meant to do!

DEVELOPING YOUR GAME PLAN

1. As you come to the end of this book, jot down two or three points that have stuck out to you. What is one you want to put into practice today?

2. What do you think is the most substantial barrier getting in the way of you fulfilling your calling? It could be fear, lack of commitment, lacking the right direction, trying too hard to be perfect on your own, being discouraged by failure, or something else. What practical steps could you take to overcome this?

3. What are some of your most significant experiences, abilities, personality traits, or passions? How do you think God might be able to fit these together into a deeper purpose? How can you be ready for whatever God has in store for you?

4. In a journal, write down what you think God might be calling you to do. This doesn't have to be your final answer! It's okay if your idea of your calling changes over time. Be bold and move forward today.

FREQUENTLY ASKED QUESTIONS

What does it take to become a sports agent?

Passion, commitment, sacrifice, determination, intense work ethic . . . and so much more. Loving sports is not enough. Being a former athlete helps, but it's still not enough. Even being a lawyer is not enough. Agents wear many hats and have to handle a broad range of situations, problems, and personalities. Agents must be able to evaluate talent, to recruit, and to communicate effectively. They must also be able to advocate, negotiate, and manage expectations. In my opinion, agents must also be compassionate and trustworthy with money.

What did you do to break into the sports agent business?

Old-fashioned hard work and lots and lots of networking! To be honest, I had no idea where to start. I was a former athlete and had always loved sports. I knew nothing about the sports industry, though, so I started from scratch. I researched NFL teams and agents. I contacted anyone and everyone, trying to get advice and develop connections. Initially, very few people responded, but I refused to quit. Just after I found out I had passed the agent certification exam, I sent out letters to every NFL front office introducing myself and asking to set up a call or meeting. Only one response came in—from a lawyer working with the Tennessee Titans. He recommended that I get in touch with one of their scouts, C. O. Brocato, who was going to be coming through Oklahoma on a scouting trip.

C. O. was pushing eighty but was sharp as a tack. We met for dinner (at 4:30 in the afternoon) at an Outback Steakhouse in Norman, Oklahoma. I told C. O. about my aspirations and questioned him endlessly about the business. I will never forget the many, many lessons he shared that day. But the thing I remember most was him pointing at me and saying, "You're going to be one of the best in the business. I can already see it." When someone else believes in you— and tells you they believe in you—it is a total game changer. C. O. would later introduce me to dozens of scouts, coaches, and other front office personnel at the NFL Combine.

My advice to you? Be a constant student of the industry. Never stop learning, and always look for opportunities to connect with others. Opportunities come through people; therefore, relationships will be key to your success.

What do you dislike about your job? What do you love most about it?

The only thing I really dislike about being an agent is the corruption and deception in the industry. The darkness can seem overwhelming at times. But it just lights an even bigger fire in me to keep fighting the good fight, knowing that truth and goodness will always win in the end!

I absolutely love my job because it allows me to serve. It is my firm belief that I was born with a purpose to pour into others and help them discover their own God-given destinies. Even the tough days and the painful moments are fulfilling when you know you are doing exactly what you were created to do.

What does a typical work day look like for you?

There is no such thing as a typical work day! But I can tell you most of my days are long, and no two are the same. During certain times of the year, I am on a plane multiple times a week. My day always starts the same way: praying, reading, and organizing my to-do list. The calls, texts, and emails start early . . . sometimes at 6:00 a.m. or earlier. I try to get in a run or workout, and then I get ready to go to the office or attack the day if I am on the road.

Depending on the time of year, I may be focused on taking care of the legal and business needs of my existing clients in the NFL, Major League Baseball, or Olympic sports while also recruiting new clients. I will also be talking to general managers, personnel directors, and pro scouts about my free agents, or I'll be talking to player development directors and coaches about my current NFL athletes. I handle everything from draft preparation to contract negotiation to relocation services. That's in addition to doing legal work, including estate planning, nonprofit organization applications, corporate formation, and providing general legal representation. I also spend a significant amount of time handling media and marketing requests plus related logistics and paperwork. In the middle of all this, I try to be as accessible as possible to each of my clients for guidance, counseling, and wisdom. Oh, and while doing all this, I am still practicing law as an Of Counsel attorney at an Oklahoma City law firm, teaching sports law as an adjunct professor, and continuing to speak and write on sports, diversity, faith, and leadership.

What are you looking for in a client?

Much of my time as an agent is spent researching and recruiting new clients, and the process looks very different from what most people imagine. My goal is to sign two to four new clients for each NFL draft. (Because of NFLPA agent regulations, I can only recruit players who are not already under contract with an agent, so I do not recruit veteran players. If a veteran wants to make a change in representation, he must contact me.)

The recruiting process starts with gathering scouting reports and other background information on thirty to forty potential clients for each draft class, whom I identify based upon athletic ability as well as character. An ideal client for me is a technically sound player with off-the-charts work ethic and leadership qualities. There are many, many factors to consider, and my research goes deep. Fortunately I've developed a tremendous network of scouts, coaches, and other trustworthy talent evaluators over the years, and I listen to what they have to say. The next step is actually getting in touch with these players or the individuals helping them make decisions about their future. Before I even reach out, I have to make sure I am properly registered with the state in which they play, as well as their school. When I do make contact, my intent is to present information and make a solid first impression that will lead to an in-person meeting. If I get that meeting, the goal is to continue building that relationship. It is imperative to earn the trust of both the player himself and his parents.

As we work through this process of discovery, the list of potential clients narrows. Sometimes a player "goes a different direction." Other times I decide to walk away from a potential signee. At the end of the regular season, a player and his family (or trusted advisers) will typically meet with their top three or four agent choices and then make a final decision. Usually I land seven or eight "final" meetings. It is always my prayer that I will sign the players I am supposed to sign. And it usually seems to work out!

Is it hard being a woman working in the NFL?

I always respond this way: It is hard for *anyone* to get into this business! Male, female, Black, white . . . doesn't matter. NFL agency is a fiercely competitive industry. However, it is all too common for people to state—often to my face—that women should not be representing NFL players. They say women could not possibly represent NFL players effectively because they never played football, they are too emotional, or they are not skilled negotiators. NONE of those are true. Sure, I've never played football, but neither have many of my colleagues. And there is significant evidence to contradict the other negative assertions about women in the industry.

Can you imagine people being told in any industry, "We aren't interested in considering you for this position because you are Hispanic/Muslim/disabled"? But somehow it is acceptable to say this to a woman? This type of discrimination is part of life for most women who work in the sports business, particularly in football, but it is not right. At the same time, because I realize exactly what I am up against, I understand the challenge. I must prove that I am not only capable of handling the duties of an NFL agent, but I am capable of doing so with excellence that exceeds the ability of my competitors.

How did COVID-19 affect you and your clients in the 2020 draft and football season?

COVID-19 has affected all of our lives in ways we never could have imagined! It has certainly been a time of fear and tragedy for many Americans and people around the globe. But we have grown and adapted, and I still believe that what the enemy means for evil God can use for good.

Just before the "shutdown" in March of 2020, I had

already started doing regular web conferences with all of the KMM clients and staff to discuss the impending player vote on the newly negotiated collective bargaining agreement between the NFL and the players' union. Once we were all confined to our homes, our regular Zoom calls became a way to maintain connection and encourage each other. Players shared tips with one another on creative ways to stay in shape while working out at home. Our KMM Advisory Council poured wisdom into all of us on these calls, and we all prayed together as a family.

Due to the pandemic, Pro Day workouts were canceled, as were pre-draft visits to teams by prospects. This made the 2020 draft process very unusual. Everything was done virtually. I had to reach out to retired NFL scouts to conduct individual workouts for my draft prospects and free agents that we could film and submit to teams. I set up Zoom interviews between players and coaches. After the draft, players were not allowed to report to their NFL facilities until training camp . . . months later than normal. Practice time was drastically reduced, and all preseason games were canceled. This meant fewer opportunities for young players to prove themselves and earn a final roster spot.

Accordingly, the League and players' union agreed on revised "COVID-19" rules, expanding practice squads and allowing more flexibility with rosters. Safety protocols have been implemented to protect players and staff as well. These include limited or no fans at games, constant testing, and limited interaction with others. Also, NFL scouts are not allowed to travel and scout players in person.

Normally I would be traveling each weekend to attend college and NFL games (at least thirty per season) and meeting with players and families. Not in 2020. As draining as it can be to travel and pour out that much, it has always been important to me to be "present" for my players and those I am seeking to represent. While I do look forward to getting back on the road eventually, I wonder if this season will have a lasting effect on my job. As agents, we've discovered just how much we can accomplish through technology. Still, I don't believe there is anything as powerful as personal interaction. At some level, that will always be part of what I do.

Do you have any negotiating tips?

Well, I don't want to give away all my tactics! But I will share these three keys:

1. Be prepared. Know your position inside and out, and be extremely thorough in your defense of that position. Also do everything you possibly can to anticipate the arguments and position of the other side. You can never be too prepared.

2. If you are absolutely digging in your heels on a particular demand—if you see it as a bottom-line nonnegotiable—know what you are willing to give up

to get it. Negotiation involves compromise. What are you willing to let go of to get what you really want?

3. Always be willing to walk away from the table. That is where you find your leverage—and leverage is power in the negotiation process.

What is your favorite memory as a sports agent?

I have several at the top of my list. Standing with the father of my first NFL client as his son ran onto the field for the first time in an NFL uniform is a moment I will never forget. (Tears were streaming down both our faces. And we went to Waffle House afterwards to celebrate!) Attending my first Super Bowl to see a client and his team hoist the Lombardi Trophy, followed by an unforgettable victory party with their families, was amazing. Finally, sitting in the greenroom at Radio City Music Hall during the 2010 NFL Draft as my client was announced as the number three overall pick was truly the thrill of a lifetime. And history was made. It may sound silly now, but one of the best parts of that particular evening was checking my phone after the fact and seeing dozens and dozens of messages from scouts, GMs, fellow agents, and others in the sports business congratulating me and my client. It was a dream come true for both of us!

ACKNOWLEDGMENTS

Thank you, first and foremost, to my merciful Savior, Jesus. My life would mean nothing—and would make no real impact—without His love and sacrifice.

To my husband, Dale: You are my toughest critic and biggest cheerleader. It is an honor to be your wife. I cannot imagine what my life would look like without you.

To John Reneau, my friend and brother in Christ who became my stepson: Your inspiration is all over this book. Thank you for your prayerful input. Every time you call to talk about what God is showing you, I realize I am hearing a sermon that will someday impact the world.

To Dale Reneau III: Your consistent wisdom, belief, and support mean the world to me. I am beyond thankful for you, and I never could have made it this far without you.

To my team at Tyndale, Jillian Schlossberg, Carol Traver, Karin Buursma, and the rest of the crew: Thank you for making this process such an amazing one! I will be forever grateful.

To my literary agents D. J. Snell and Crosland Stuart: Thank you for guiding me through this process and for being patient with me as I learned to be the client instead of the agent. Also to Todd Starowitz, who encouraged me to start this journey years ago. I will never forget where I was the day we first spoke about this book.

To Mr. Huggins, the high school English teacher (and football coach) who taught me to write *and* taught me to love writing: You will never know the depths of your impact on my life and the lives of your countless students.

To Andy Andrews: Your books changed my life, and your friendship has inspired me even in the darkest of days. I am forever grateful and hope to make you proud.

To Chris Harrison: You've always been there for me, my friend. Thank you for your feedback and for supporting me through all the highs and lows of life. I could not ask for a better friend.

To the many friends and family members who have poured into my life over the years: I hope you know how important you are to me and to the world around you. I know I would not be the same without your impact.

To the entire KMM Family—every client and person who has believed in me. It is because of you that I have a story to tell. You are all world-changers. I know this because you changed my world!

NOTES

INTRODUCTION
1. *Jerry Maguire*, directed by Cameron Crowe (Culver City, CA: TriStar Pictures, 1996).

CHAPTER 7: DON'T BE AFRAID
1. Jon Acuff, Twitter, December 11, 2019.

CHAPTER 8: YOU ARE MORE THAN WHAT YOU DO
1. "How an MMA Fighter Found Salvation among the Pygmies," Yahoo! Sports, March 24, 2015, https://sports.yahoo.com/news/how-an -mma-fighter-found-salvation-among-the-pygmies-203846372.html ?guccounter=1.
2. "How an MMA Fighter Found Salvation."

CHAPTER 9: JUST TRUST GOD
1. "I Give Myself Away," Sam Hinn and William McDowell, copyright 2008 Delivery Room Publishing.
2. Tim Kizziar, as quoted in Francis Chan, *Crazy Love* (Colorado Springs: David C. Cook, 2013), 92.
3. Rick Warren, *The Purpose Driven Life* (Grand Rapids, MI: Zondervan, 2002), 73.
4. Warren, *The Purpose*, 21.

ABOUT THE AUTHOR

Kelli Masters is the founder, CEO, and chief player agent for KMM Sports, and she is widely recognized as one of the most influential women in sports business. She has represented more professional athletes than any woman in the industry, having served as agent/contract adviser to players in every NFL draft since 2006 as well as numerous players in the MLB draft. In 2010, she made history as the first woman to represent a top-five pick in the NFL draft. Kelli is a former National and World Champion baton twirler and was also Miss Oklahoma 1997. She is an attorney and has served as an adjunct professor at Oklahoma City University and Oklahoma Christian University, teaching sports law. Kelli and her husband, Dale, live in Oklahoma City.